You,

Yes YOU,

Can Teach Someone

to Read

A Step by Step How-To Book

Lucille Tessier Chagnon

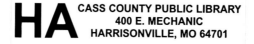

First published by AuthorHouse 12/17/04

ISBN: 1-4184-9873-4 (e)
ISBN: 1-4184-9874-2 (sc)

Library of Congress Control Number: 2004195239

Printed in the United States of America
Bloomington, Indiana

This book is printed on acid-free paper.

authorHOUSE

1663 LIBERTY DRIVE, SUITE 200
BLOOMINGTON, INDIANA 47403
(800) 839-8640
www.authorhouse.com

THE TUTORING LOG
MINDMAPS
AND ALPHABET STRIPS
AT THE END OF THIS BOOK
MAY BE REPRODUCED WITHOUT PERMISSION.

ENDORSEMENTS

I HAVE NEVER SEEN SUCH A CONCISE STEP BY STEP APPROACH TO TEACHING LITERACY, NOR ONE WHICH IS SO INSPIRING AND WELCOMING. HOW CAN WE *NOT* TAKE ON THIS CHALLENGE FOR OUR SOCIETY? –Beverly L. Stewart, M.Ed.
President/Director, Back to Basics Learning Dynamics, Inc.

This step by step how-to book on teaching someone to read is splendid. The text is clear, economical, to the point. The procedure is innovative, intriguing, provocative, and absolutely sound, founded on solid learning principles and a keen understanding of the blocks to learning and how to avoid them. The work holds real promise.
–Joseph Chilton Pearce, author, *Magical Child*

Lucille Chagnon holds forth the vision of wiping out low literacy in our lifetime. This book goes way beyond a mere vision. It suggests how-to in ways that are authentic and humanizing. Lucille demonstrates much of what current brain-mind research has discovered is involved in effective teaching and learning. The strategies and techniques presented in this book can indeed make the vision of wiping out low literacy a reality.
–David G. Lazear, author, *OutSmart Yourself! 16 Proven Strategies for Becoming Smarter Than You Think You Are*

I have skimmed through the materials, stopped to read, marveled over pages and generally overall enjoyed every bit of what has been produced. It is based on good theory; it is interesting, clever and engaging. What Lucille Chagnon is doing is important, and I want to help.
–Bernice E. Cullinan, Ed.D.
Past President, International Reading Association

You, Yes YOU, Can Teach Someone To Read is an intelligent approach to reading instruction. If used as presented, many youngsters and older people can unlock the door to meaning. –Miriam T. Chaplin, Ed.D.
Professor Emerita of Education, Rutgers University
Past President, National Council of Teachers of English

This is an excellent train-the-trainer handbook for literacy capacity-building. At a time when ramping up literacy is a key national education goal, Lucille's book serves as a rich and user-friendly resource for community-based literacy efforts. She offers practical, research-based strategies for teaching reading and for coaching new readers to become literacy tutors themselves. She encourages a sensitive, facilitative approach that builds upon the learner's strengths and authentic life experience, models reflective practice, and affirms the unfolding possibilities of exciting partnerships in literacy skill development. –Marilyn Crocker, Ed.D.
President, Crocker & Associates, Inc., Education Consultant

DEDICATION

To my sons, Dave and Dan,
and to Laura Esposito.
When you were kids
you showed me what was possible
and got me started on a whole new path.

A blessed thing happened to me
as a beginning teacher—
I had students who taught me well.
The same blessings continue to come to me
every year that I teach.
--Bernice E. Cullinan

CONTENTS

THE LETTERS OF THE ALPHABET
THAT FRAME THE ALTERNATE PAGES
ARE THE BUILDING BLOCKS THAT HAVE FREIGHTED
THE WISDOM OF MEN AND WOMEN ACROSS THE CENTURIES.

THE OPEN SPACE ON THOSE PAGES IS AN INVITATION
TO ADD YOUR OWN THOUGHTS, INSIGHTS, PLANS,
QUOTES, TITLES OF BOOKS, POEMS:
IN SHORT, YOUR OWN WISDOM.

TO SHARE YOUR INSIGHTS AND QUESTIONS
WITH OTHERS
JOIN THE DIALOGUE AT
www.teachtwo.net

TO DUPLICATE THE MICROSOFT SMALL CAPS FONT
USED THROUGHOUT THIS BOOK
ON THE TOOLBAR (NEXT TO **B** *I* U̲) CLICK ABC
OR
UNDER FORMAT
CLICK FONT / **ARIAL** / SMALL CAPS.

1

A B C D E F G H I J K L M N O P Q R S T U V W X Y Z

A
B
C
D
E
F
G
H
I
J
K
L
M
N
O
P
Q
R
S
T
U
V
W
X
Y
Z

THROUGHOUT HISTORY,
THE REALLY FUNDAMENTAL CHANGES HAVE COME ABOUT
NOT FROM THE DICTATES OF GOVERNMENTS
AND THE RESULTS OF BATTLES
BUT THROUGH VAST NUMBERS OF PEOPLE
CHANGING THEIR MIND—
SOMETIMES ONLY A LITTLE BIT.
--*WILLIS HARMAN*

2

OVERVIEW AND CHALLENGE

A VIABLE SOLUTION TO THE MASSIVE PROBLEM OF LOW LITERACY:

TURN THE COMMUNITY OF NEED INTO THE COMMUNITY OF SERVICE.

TURN WILLING NEW READERS, YOUNG AND OLD,
INTO COMMUNITY-BASED TUTORS.

EACH OF YOU TEACH TWO!

THIS UNIQUE APPROACH IS BASED ON THE FOLLOWING PREMISES SYNERGISTICALLY COMBINED:

- IN A PRINT-SATURATED SOCIETY LIKE THE UNITED STATES, THERE ARE NO NON-READERS. THERE ARE, HOWEVER, MILLIONS OF HESITANT READERS WHO CANNOT READ WELL ENOUGH TO FUNCTION FULLY IN OUR SOCIETY AND REALIZE THEIR FULL POTENTIAL. MILLIONS OF PEOPLE WHO CAN RECOGNIZE **STOP, GO, BANK,** AND **BUS** WERE NEVER SHOWN HOW EASY IT IS TO BEGIN TO BUILD A READING FOUNDATION ON THOSE SIMPLE WORDS.

- ALL HUMAN BEINGS ARE GIFTED; BUT WE ALL USE A SMALL PERCENTAGE OF OUR BRAIN POWER. VAST NUMBERS OF ADULTS, WHO CLAIM THEY CANNOT READ, LIVE CARING AND PRODUCTIVE LIVES AND FIND AMAZINGLY CREATIVE WAYS TO COMPENSATE FOR THEIR INABILITY TO DECODE PRINT.

- CHILDREN AND ADULTS WHO ARE TOLD THAT THEY ARE LEARNING DISABLED OR UNABLE TO FOCUS MAY COME TO BELIEVE THAT THEY ARE INFERIOR—AND EVEN MORE SO IF THEIR TEACHERS AND FAMILY DO NOT UNDERSTAND THE GIFT OF LEARNING DIFFERENCES AND MISTAKENLY BUY INTO THE NEGATIVE LABELS.

- IT IS POSSIBLE TO BRING STUDENTS WITH LEARNING DIFFERENCES UP TO GRADE LEVEL IN READING AND EVEN TO TEACH INDIVIDUALS WITH IQS IN THE 30S TO READ WITH UNDERSTANDING AND ENTHUSIASM. THE WELL-DOCUMENTED WORK OF DR. RENÉE FULLER PROVED THAT OVER 30 YEARS AGO. WITH FULLER'S MULTI-SENSORY SYSTEM OF CAPITAL LETTERS THERE ARE NO REVERSALS.

- THE MOST IMPORTANT FACTOR IN TEACHING SOMEONE TO READ IS HEARTFELT LISTENING. ANXIETY CAUSES THE BRAIN TO DOWNSHIFT. AUTHENTIC LISTENING DISPELS ANXIETY AND CREATES SAFE SPACE WHICH ACCELERATES LEARNING. WHEN RELUCTANT READERS FEEL SAFE, THEY DO NOT HAVE TO APOLOGIZE OR PRETEND. AN EXCITING NEW WORLD OF LEARNING OPENS UP WHERE PAST PERFORMANCE MAKES LITTLE DIFFERENCE.

- THE MOST POWERFUL TEACHING RESOURCE IS THE LIFE EXPERIENCE OF NEW READERS. ONCE THEY FEEL SAFE AND BEGIN TO REVEAL WHAT INTERESTS THEM MOST, WORDS ABOUT THINGS THEY LOVE WILL BECOME SIGHT WORDS ON WHICH TO BUILD A READING VOCABULARY. AS THE MOTIVATION TO LEARN BECOMES SELF-DIRECTED AND SELF-REINFORCING, THEY MAY DISCOVER ALL KINDS OF BOOKS THAT CAN FEED THEIR INTERESTS AND FIRE THEIR IMAGINATION.

- WE ALL LEARN BEST WHEN WE TEACH SOMEONE ELSE; THAT IS ALSO TRUE IN LEARNING TO READ FLUENTLY. EVEN YOUNG READERS CAN TEACH OTHER CHILDREN FROM SCRATCH, PROVIDING THEY BELIEVE THAT THEY CAN AND HAVE ACCESS TO SIMPLE METHODS AND A MENTOR, THEIR FORMER TUTOR, TO GUIDE THEM THROUGH THE PROCESS—BEFORE, DURING, AND AFTER EACH TUTORING SESSION—UNTIL THEY ARE READY TO TRY IT ON THEIR OWN.

- A VAST CORPS OF POTENTIAL LITERACY TUTORS OF ALL AGES—TODAY'S HESITANT READERS—EXISTS IN THE VERY SCHOOLS AND NEIGHBORHOODS WHERE TUTORS ARE MOST NEEDED. MANY ADULTS ARE EMBARRASSED TO WORK WITH VOLUNTEERS FROM OUTSIDE THEIR COMMUNITY. THAT CONDITION CAN BE REVERSED IF INTERESTED INDIVIDUALS LEARN HOW TO TUTOR THEIR OWN CHILDREN, SIBLINGS, FRIENDS. ONE COMMITTED AND CREDIBLE COMMUNITY-BASED TUTOR, EAGER TO TRAIN OTHERS TO PASS IT ON, COULD START A LANDSLIDE.

- ENCOURAGING NEW READERS TO TEACH TWO OTHERS IN THEIR LIFETIME CREATES A GEOMETRIC PROGRESSION OF LEARNING. FRANK LAUBACH'S CALL TO LITERACY IN THE LAST HALF OF THE 20TH CENTURY, *EACH ONE TEACH ONE*, CATALYZED THE DISSEMINATION OF EXCELLENT METHODS AND THE CREATION OF A DEDICATED WORLDWIDE CORPS OF VOLUNTEERS, AS DID THE GROUNDBREAKING WORK OF RUTH COLVIN, FOUNDER OF LITERACY VOLUNTEERS OF AMERICA (LVA). THE CALL TO UNIVERSAL LITERACY FOR THE 21ST CENTURY BUILDS ON THAT PAST AND AMPLIFIES IT, HANDING THE SKILLS OF TEACHING—AND EVENTUALLY, MENTORING—OVER TO WILLING NEW READERS, YOUNG OR OLD. NOW, *EACH OF YOU TEACH TWO!*

- AUTHENTIC PARTNERSHIPS PROMOTE HEALING, INCREASE SELF-RELIANCE AND CREATIVITY ALL AROUND, AND STRENGTHEN COMMUNITY LEADERSHIP. TO BEGIN TO WIPE OUT LOW LITERACY, WE MUST FOREGO ANY HIERARCHICAL, BEGGAR-AT-THE-GATE PERSPECTIVE, ANY TRACE OF A PROPRIETARY, DOGMATIC MENTALITY. WE CAN AND MUST DEVELOP MUTUALLY ENRICHING PARTNERSHIPS BETWEEN THE HAVES AND THE HAVE-NOTS AND AMONG SERVICE PROVIDERS AS WELL. YOUNG AND OLD, DEGREED AND CERTIFIED OR NOT, AS WE HELP EACH OTHER LEARN, WE ALL GROW IN THE SHARING.

- IF WE BUT FIND THE WILL, THE SIMPLE LEARNING TECHNOLOGY EXISTS TO BEGIN TO WIPE OUT FUNCTIONAL ILLITERACY IN OUR LIFETIME. AS LITERACY PROVIDERS BUILD MORE AND MORE COLLABORATIVE RELATIONSHIPS WITH EACH OTHER AND WITH COMMUNITY-BASED TUTORS, WE CAN TAP THE SYNERGY OF PARTNERSHIP. THOUGH UNHERALDED, SEPTIMA CLARK AND MYLES HORTON PROVED THAT CONCLUSIVELY IN THE DEEP SOUTH OF THE 1950S WITH HUNDREDS OF CITIZENSHIP SCHOOLS THAT QUIETLY PAVED THE WAY AND PREPARED A PEOPLE FOR THE CIVIL RIGHTS MOVEMENT OF THE 1960S.

IF WE CARE ENOUGH AND DARE ENOUGH, WE CAN

TURN THE COMMUNITY OF NEED INTO THE COMMUNITY OF SERVICE.

WORKING TOGETHER WE CAN BEGIN TO WIPE OUT LOW LITERACY.

EACH OF YOU TEACH TWO!

A B C D E F G H I J K L M N O P Q R S T U V W X Y Z

A
B
C
D
E
F
G
H
I
J
K
L
M
N
O
P
Q
R
S
T
U
V
W
X
Y
Z

AND THE PURPOSE OF LIFE, AFTER ALL, IS TO LIVE IT,
TO TASTE THE EXPERIENCE TO THE UTMOST,
TO REACH OUT EAGERLY AND WITHOUT FEAR
FOR NEWER AND RICHER EXPERIENCE.
YOU CAN DO THAT ONLY IF YOU HAVE CURIOSITY,
AN UNQUENCHABLE SPIRIT OF ADVENTURE...
YOU MUST DO THE THING YOU CANNOT DO.
--*ELEANOR ROOSEVELT*

You, Yes YOU, Can Teach Someone to Read

WHO CAN TEACH?

ANYONE
WHO CAN

    ...LISTEN

    LAUGH
    LACK PRETENSE
    LATCH ON TO POSSIBILITY

        ...LISTEN

        LET GO
        LEARN WITH
        LIVE IN THE MOMENT

            ...LISTEN

            LEVEL WITH
            LINGER OVER
            LIVE WITH THE QUESTIONS

                ...LISTEN

                LIGHT A FIRE
                LICK THE BLUES
                LOVE LEARNING

  ...LISTEN
      ...LISTEN
          ...LISTEN
              ...LISTEN

WHO CAN TEACH?

    YOU, YES YOU, CAN TEACH SOMEONE TO READ.

A B C D E F G H I J K L M N O P Q R S T U V W X Y Z

A
B
C
D
E
F
G
H
I
J
K
L
M
N
O
P
Q
R
S
T
U
V
W
X
Y
Z

IT SHOULD BE POSSIBLE FOR YOUNG PEOPLE
TO LEARN TO READ AT HOME
JUST AS THEY LEARN WALKING AND TALKING
FOR THE MOST PART AT HOME.
--HERBERT KOHL

<u>WHO</u> ARE YOU?

IF YOU ARE DRAWN TO THIS BOOK
YOU ARE PERHAPS

A MOM, DAD
SISTER, BROTHER

        AUNT, UNCLE
        LONG LOST COUSIN

                A SITTER, NEIGHBOR
                GRANDPARENT, FRIEND

                        A CLERK, A STYLIST
                        A COACH, A MUSICIAN

                A CAFETERIA WORKER
                AN ANIMAL LOVER

        A SCHOOL PRINCIPAL
        A SECURITY GUARD

AN AVID READER
A LIBRARIAN…

SOMEONE WHOSE BRIGHT KIDS
ARE HAVING A TOUGH TIME IN SCHOOL;

SOMEONE WHOSE LIFE WAS CHANGED BY READING
LOOKING FOR AN OPPORTUNITY TO SIMPLY PASS IT ON;

SOMEONE WHOSE COMPANY ENCOURAGES VOLUNTEERISM
LOOKING FOR A CHANCE TO JOIN OR EXPAND THE ENDEAVOR;

SOMEONE WHO IS TIRED OF THE SAME OLD SAME OLD
WHO BELIEVES THAT EVERYONE CAN LEARN;

SOMEONE WHO CARES
SOMEONE WHO DARES
SOMEONE WHO…

                THE LIST IS ENDLESS.

A B C D E F G H I J K L M N O P Q R S T U V W X Y Z

A
B
C
D
E
F
G
H
I
J
K
L
M
N
O
P
Q
R
S
T
U
V
W
X
Y
Z

I CAME HERE TO SING
AND FOR YOU TO SING WITH ME.
--*PABLO NERUDA*

10

IN OTHER WORDS…

IF YOU CAN BE

A GUIDE

      A COACH

           A GIVING FRIEND

                A FELLOW LEARNER

                     AN ENTHUSIASTIC SUPPORTER…

IF YOU CAN BE A SOURCE OF ENCOURAGEMENT

                    AND ENLIGHTENMENT…

THEN YOU CAN BE

A GENUINE LEARNING PARTNER…

SOMEONE WHO
          JOURNEYS WITH…

SOMEONE WHO
          DISCOVERS WITH…

SOMEONE WHO
          LEARNS WITH…

SOMEONE WHO
          LEARNS FROM
                A LEARNING PARTNER…

THEN BOTH OF YOU CAN BE

      GENUINE LEARNING PARTNERS

      LEARNING TOGETHER FROM EACH OTHER.

A B C D E F G H I J K L M N O P Q R S T U V W X Y Z

A
B
C
D
E
F
G
H
I
J
K
L
M
N
O
P
Q
R
S
T
U
V
W
X
Y
Z

WISDOM ISN'T FOUND BY PILING UP KNOWLEDGE.
RATHER, IT IS THE FINDING
OF HIDDEN PATTERNS OF MEANING AND BEAUTY
THAT CAN RENEW INDIVIDUALS
AND REUNITE THE COMMUNITY.
--*MICHAEL MEAD*

<u>WHOM</u> CAN YOU TEACH?

AN ARTIST
      A BROTHER OR SISTER
            A CHURCH MEMBER

A DROP-OUT
      AN EIGHTH GRADER
            A FRIEND

A GRANDPARENT
      A HOMELESS PERSON
            AN IMMIGRANT

A JUVENILE ON PROBATION
      A KINDERGARTNER
            A LIFER IN PRISON

A MOTHER OR FATHER
      A NEIGHBOR
            AN OLD-TIMER

A PREGNANT TEEN
      A QUARTERBACK
            A RESILIENT SURVIVOR

A SCOUT
      A TRUMPET PLAYER
            AN UNCLE OR AUNT

A VOCAL TEAMMATE
      A WILD AND CRAZY GUY
            AN EX-OFFENDER

A YARN-SPINNER
      A ZEALOT

JUST ABOUT ANYONE WHO'S WILLING TO GIVE IT A TRY
FOR AT LEAST A SESSION OR TWO.

A B C D E F G H I J K L M N O P Q R S T U V W X Y Z

A
B
C
D
E
F
G
H
I
J
K
L
M
N
O
P
Q
R
S
T
U
V
W
X
Y
Z

**WE ARE ALL FACED
WITH A SERIES OF GREAT OPPORTUNITIES
BRILLIANTLY DISGUISED
AS IMPOSSIBLE SITUATIONS.**
--CHARLES SWINDOLL

<u>WHERE</u> CAN YOU FIND A LEARNING PARTNER?

PERHAPS THERE IS SOMEONE IN **YOUR FAMILY**
WHO IS STYMIED BY THE PRINTED WORD
AFRAID OF OR UNINTERESTED IN BOOKS.

ASK THE PEOPLE AT **YOUR LOCAL LIBRARY** FOR LEADS.

REACH OUT TO **ESTABLISHED ORGANIZATIONS** LIKE
PROLITERACY AMERICA
THE U.S. PROGRAMS DIVISION OF PROLITERACY WORLDWIDE. *

IT'S WISE TO WORK WITH ESTABLISHED PROGRAMS
AND TO ADD THEIR LONG EXPERIENCE, SAVVY, AND SUPPORT
TO WHAT YOU ALREADY KNOW
—WHICH MAY BE MUCH MORE THAN YOU THINK YOU KNOW—
AND TO WHAT YOU WILL HAVE LEARNED IN THIS BOOK.

REACH OUT TO **SCHOOLS**.
MANY PRINCIPALS AND TEACHERS WELCOME CLASSROOM TUTORS.
TALK TO YOUR CHILDREN'S OR GRANDCHILDREN'S TEACHERS.

MANY SCHOOLS HAVE **AFTER-SCHOOL PROGRAMS**
AS DO BOYS' AND GIRLS' CLUBS, AS WELL AS
COMMUNITY AND NEIGHBORHOOD CENTERS.

INQUIRE ABOUT **ADULT SCHOOL PROGRAMS**:
ADULT BASIC EDUCATION / **ABE**
ENGLISH AS A SECOND LANGUAGE / **ESL**.

RELIGIOUS DENOMINATIONS OFTEN SPONSOR
EDUCATIONAL PROGRAMS FOR CHILDREN
YOUTH
ADULTS.

MANY **ORGANIZATIONS IN YOUR COMMUNITY**
MIGHT WELCOME YOUR TUTORING SERVICES
ON A REGULAR BASIS.

* PROLITERACY WORLDWIDE WAS FORMED BY THE MERGER OF LAUBACH INTERNATIONAL
AND LITERACY VOLUNTEERS OF AMERICA, INC. (LVA). THE OFFICE IN YOUR COMMUNITY
MAY HAVE KEPT ONE OF THOSE ORIGINAL NAMES.

A B C D E F G H I J K L M N O P Q R S T U V W X Y Z

A
B
C
D
E
F
G
H
I
J
K
L
M
N
O
P
Q
R
S
T
U
V
W
X
Y
Z

SOME OF US CANNOT IMAGINE WHAT OUR TALENTS ARE
UNTIL WE ARE FORCED BY CIRCUMSTANCES OR CHOICE
TO SURRENDER THE COMFORTS OF HOME
AND MAKE OUR WAY IN ALIEN TERRITORY,
USING ONLY THE TOOLS WE CARRY WITH US.
--HOWARD FIGLER

<u>WHERE</u> CAN YOU TEACH?

YOU CAN TEACH…

AT A DESK
AT A TABLE

    ON A BENCH
    IN A PUBLIC PARK

        IN A LIBRARY
        IN A CAFETERIA

            IN A GROUP HOME
            IN A RETIREMENT HOME

            IN A COMMUNITY MEETING SPACE
            AT A MOSQUE, SYNAGOGUE, CHURCH

        IN A SHELTER FOR THE HOMELESS
        AT A NEIGHBORHOOD CENTER

    IN A PRISON OR HALFWAY HOUSE
    IN A JUVENILE INSTITUTION

IN A SCHOOL NEAR YOUR HOME
IN A KINDERGARTEN.

WHERE CAN YOU TEACH?

IN LOTS OF PLACES.

JUST MAKE SURE THAT IT IS SOMEWHERE **PUBLIC**

    WHERE YOU ARE NOT ALONE

WHERE YOU CAN HAVE REASONABLE **PRIVACY**

AND WHERE BOTH YOU AND YOUR LEARNING PARTNER

    FEEL TOTALLY **COMFORTABLE.**

A B C D E F G H I J K L M N O P Q R S T U V W X Y Z

A
B
C
D
E
F
G
H
I
J
K
L
M
N
O
P
Q
R
S
T
U
V
W
X
Y
Z

THE UNUSED MIND
THAT LIES BEHIND YOUR OPEN EYES
IS THE NEXT GREAT ENERGY RESOURCE
AFTER THE ATOM.
--*DORELLE HEISEL*

<u>WHEN</u> CAN YOU TEACH?

WHEN SOMEONE IS…

AWKWARD
 BEWILDERED
  CONVINCED THEY'RE STUPID
   DISCOURAGED

EAGER TO LEARN
 FED UP WITH FAILURE
  GETTING NOWHERE

HUNGRY FOR KNOWLEDGE
 IN RECOVERY
  JUST RARIN' TO GO
   KICKING OLD HABITS

LONGING TO NOT BE LABELED
 MIXED UP
  NERVOUS
   OPEN TO LEARNING
    PASSIVE

QUESTIONING
 RESTLESS
  SAD IN SCHOOL

TEACHER-PROOF
 UNSURE
  VYING FOR ATTENTION

WAITING FOR GODOT
 EXHAUSTED

YOUNG AT HEART OR NOT
 ZANY ENOUGH TO TRY.

NOW YOU'VE SAID YOUR ABCS
WHOM COULD YOU TEACH
HOW TO READ?

A B C D E F G H I J K L M N O P Q R S T U V W X Y Z

A
B
C
D
E
F
G
H
I
J
K
L
M
N
O
P
Q
R
S
T
U
V
W
X
Y
Z

GREAT AND SUCCESSFUL PEOPLE...
WERE ENCOURAGED IN THEIR DREAMS
BY SOMEONE THEY CONSIDERED IMPORTANT,
WHILE THE UNSUCCESSFUL WERE MADE TO FEEL
THEIR DREAMS WERE FOOLISH AND IMPRACTICAL.
--PETER KLINE

WHY TEACH SOMEONE TO READ?

CAN YOU IMAGINE
THE THRILL OF SEEING YOUR LEARNING PARTNERS
CHANGE THEIR RELATIONSHIP TO THE PRINTED WORD
AND TO THEIR OWN CAPACITY TO LEARN
BEFORE YOUR VERY EYES?

YOU WILL HAVE THE PRIVILEGE OF OBSERVING
HOW READING CAN CHANGE THE STORY THAT INDIVIDUALS TELL
ABOUT THEMSELVES AND ABOUT THEIR WORLD.

YOU WILL SEE FOR YOURSELF HOW LEARNING FROM THE GUT
MAY BEGIN TO TRANSFORM YOUR LEARNING PARTNERS
IN ANY ONE OF MANY POSSIBLE WAYS:

FROM		
	APATHY	TO **Z**EST
	BOREDOM	TO **Y**EARNING
	CAUTION	TO E**X**CITEMENT
	DAYDREAMING	TO **W**RITING
	EXCUSES	TO **V**ISUALIZING
	FEAR	TO **U**RGENCY
	GLIB ANSWERS	TO **T**OUGH CHOICES
	HOLDING BACK	TO **S**EARCHING
	INERTIA	TO **R**EADINESS
	JUMBLED FEELINGS	TO **Q**UESTIONING
	KICKS	TO **P**LUCK
	LOW ENERGY	TO **O**PENNESS
	MANIPULATING	TO **N**UDGING

A B C D E F G H I J K L M N O P Q R S T U V W X Y Z

A
B
C
D
E
F
G
H
I
J
K
L
M
N
O
P
Q
R
S
T
U
V
W
X
Y
Z

SURVIVAL
IS LEARNING TO SWIM
IN STRANGE WATER.
--FRANK HERBERT

22

HOW DO YOU GET STARTED?

AGAIN, ONE OF THE BEST WAYS TO GET STARTED
IS TO WORK THROUGH ESTABLISHED LITERACY ORGANIZATIONS
LIKE **ProLiteracy America**.
CHECK OUT THE WEALTH OF INFORMATION ON THEIR WEBSITE. *

BUT ALSO LOOK INTO OTHER **LOCAL LITERACY GROUPS**.
GET COPIES OF THEIR BROCHURES AND OTHER LITERATURE.
ASK ABOUT THEIR TRAINING PROGRAMS
AND THEIR BROADER AFFILIATIONS.

WORKING WITH AN ESTABLISHED ORGANIZATION
YIELDS MANY BENEFITS FOR YOU
                     FOR THEM
                           FOR YOUR LEARNING PARTNERS.

- THEIR METHODS AND MATERIALS WILL ADD TO AND REINFORCE WHAT YOU HAVE LEARNED THROUGH YOUR OWN EXPERIENCE AND IN THIS BOOK.

- WHEN YOU ATTEND THE REQUIRED TRAINING SESSIONS YOU WILL MEET OTHER TUTORS, OTHER COLLEAGUES.

- THEIR STAFF WILL BE THERE TO ANSWER YOUR QUESTIONS AND PROVIDE SUGGESTIONS WHEN YOU NEED HELP.

- THEY WILL FIND LEARNING PARTNERS FOR YOU, AND THEY MAY RECOMMEND PUBLIC SITES WHERE YOU CAN MEET REGULARLY.

- WORKING UNDER THEIR AUSPICES WILL PROVIDE A MEASURE OF ONGOING ACCOUNTABILITY, WHICH WILL INCREASE YOUR OWN COMFORT LEVEL.

- REPRESENTING AN ESTABLISHED ORGANIZATION WILL ADD TO YOUR CREDENTIALS AND CREDIBILITY IN THE EYES OF YOUR LEARNING PARTNERS AND THEIR FAMILIES.

- AS DEDICATED AS THEIR STAFF AND TUTORS ARE, EVEN THE BEST LITERACY ORGANIZATIONS ARE ABLE TO REACH FEW OF THE INDIVIDUALS WHO WOULD NEED THEIR SERVICES—SOME SAY AS LITTLE AS 2 TO 10%. THEY WELCOME ANYONE WHO CAN HELP EXTEND THEIR REACH.

* SEE **A READING LIST AND SOME WEBSITES**.

A B C D E F G H I J K L M N O P Q R S T U V W X Y Z

A
B
C
D
E
F
G
H
I
J
K
L
M
N
O
P
Q
R
S
T
U
V
W
X
Y
Z

IF YOU ASK ME
WHAT I'VE COME TO DO IN THIS WORLD,
I REPLY,
"I'M HERE TO LIVE ALOUD."
--EMILE ZOLA

<u>HOW</u> DO YOU REALLY GET STARTED?

IF YOU ARE GOING TO WORK WITH SOMEONE YOU DO NOT KNOW
DECIDE BEFOREHAND
WHETHER YOU WANT TO BE CALLED BY YOUR FIRST NAME
OR WHETHER YOU WANT TO BE CALLED MR., MS., MRS.

THEN WHEN YOU MEET, TAKE TIME TO GET TO KNOW EACH OTHER.

DEPENDING ON YOUR LEARNING PARTNER'S AGE
ASK QUESTIONS SUCH AS:

> "WHAT MADE YOU DECIDE
> TO WORK ONE-ON-ONE WITH SOMEONE?
> WHAT DID (OR DO) YOU LIKE MOST/LEAST ABOUT SCHOOL?
> WHAT DO YOU WANT TO LEARN MOST?"

EXPLAIN BRIEFLY WHERE *YOU* ARE COMING FROM:

> HOW YOU FEEL ABOUT WORKING ONE-ON-ONE…
> WHY YOU USE THE TERM LEARNING PARTNER AND NOT TUTOR…
> WHAT YOU EXPECT TO LEARN…

IF IT'S ALL NEW TO YOU, BE HONEST:

> "I'VE NEVER DONE THIS BEFORE."

AND BE OPEN:

> "WE'LL LEARN TOGETHER, FROM EACH OTHER.
> IF I DON'T KNOW SOMETHING, I'LL SAY SO
> AND WE'LL FIGURE IT OUT TOGETHER.
>
> IF EITHER OF US IS UNCOMFORTABLE, WE'LL SAY SO.
> IF IT'S NOT WORKING, WE'LL TRY A DIFFERENT APPROACH."

IF YOU BOTH AGREE TO GIVE IT A TRY
CONFIRM THE DAY, TIME, AND PUBLIC PLACE
WHERE YOU WILL MEET.

THEN GET STARTED ON YOUR FIRST PROJECT TOGETHER:

A MINDMAP ABOUT THEM.

A B C D E F G H I J K L M N O P Q R S T U V W X Y Z

A
B
C
D
E
F
G
H
I
J
K
L
M
N
O
P
Q
R
S
T
U
V
W
X
Y
Z

WE ARE ALL STORYTELLERS,
AND THE STORY THAT CONSUMES US MOST
IS THE ONE WE TELL OURSELVES
ABOUT OUR OWN LIVES.
--PENNEY PEIRCE

AT YOUR FIRST SESSION TOGETHER, YOUR LEARNING PARTNERS
WILL BE MORE COMFORTABLE TALKING ABOUT THEMSELVES
IF YOU LET THEM GET TO KNOW YOU A BIT FIRST.

ONE OPTION IS TO DO IT ON A MINDMAP LIKE THE ONE BELOW.
YOU CAN MAKE A PHOTOCOPY OF THE ONE AT THE END OF THIS BOOK
OR SIMPLY TAKE A BLANK SHEET OF PAPER
TURN IT SIDEWAYS AND DRAW ONE YOURSELF. *

TO GET THE BALL ROLLING
PRINT YOUR NAME IN CAPS IN THE SMALL MIDDLE OVAL
AS YOU START TO TELL YOUR LEARNING PARTNER A BIT ABOUT YOURSELF:
    WHERE YOU LIVE
    SOMETHING ABOUT YOUR FAMILY
    YOUR FRIENDS
    YOUR FAVORITE THINGS.

CHAT AS YOU ADD LINES CLOCKWISE FROM ONE O'CLOCK
AND AS YOU PUT WORDS ON THE LINES.

TURN YOUR CREATION INTO A CONVERSATION, BUT KEEP IT BRIEF.
YOUR LEARNING PARTNERS ARE, AND MUST REMAIN, THE FOCUS.
YOUR ANECDOTES WILL PREPARE THEM FOR THE NEXT MINDMAP
THEIR FIRST—WHICH WILL BEGIN TO INTRODUCE YOU
TO THEIR LIFE
        THEIR FAMILY AND FRIENDS
            THEIR INTERESTS
                THEIR STORIES.

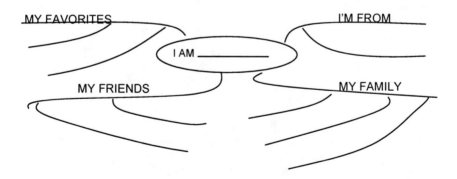

MY FAVORITES   I'M FROM

I AM _____

MY FRIENDS   MY FAMILY

* SO THAT YOU CAN READ THE MAP HEAD-ON AND NOT HAVE TO TURN IT AROUND, AVOID
  VERTICAL OR SHARP DIAGONAL LINES.

A B C D E F G H I J K L M N O P Q R S T U V W X Y Z

A
B
C
D
E
F
G
H
I
J
K
L
M
N
O
P
Q
R
S
T
U
V
W
X
Y
Z

I HAVE NEVER DRAWN AN ARTIFICIAL LINE
BETWEEN TEACHING AND LEARNING.
A TEACHER, OF COURSE,
SHOULD KNOW MORE THAN HIS PUPIL.
BUT FOR ME, TO TEACH IS TO LEARN.
--*PABLO CASALS*

A MINDMAP IS A WEB
>   A CLUSTER
>   A BRAIN-DUMP
>   A GRAPHIC ORGANIZER
>   A SELF-ORGANIZING BRAINSTORM.

IF YOU STICK TO THE FACTS
THERE ARE NO RIGHT OR WRONG ANSWERS;
AND WERE YOU TO DO ANOTHER MINDMAP
ON THE SAME TOPIC AT ANOTHER TIME
IT WOULD BE SOMEWHAT DIFFERENT.

IF YOU HAVE NEVER SEEN OR CREATED A MINDMAP BEFORE
YOU WILL DISCOVER
THAT IT'S AN UNBELIEVABLY SIMPLE AND EFFECTIVE WAY
TO TEACH YOUR LEARNING PARTNERS
HOW TO SUMMARIZE A FAVORITE BOOK
>   A FILM
>   A SPECIAL DAY
>   ANYTHING UNDER THE SUN.

IN FACT, A MINDMAP IS A TIME-SAVING TOOL
THAT YOU MIGHT WANT TO USE YOURSELF
TO PLAN YOUR SESSIONS WITH YOUR LEARNING PARTNER.

(MINDMAPPING IS ALSO A TOOL YOU CAN BRING TO WORK OR SCHOOL
TO GREATLY SIMPLIFY AND ORGANIZE REPORTS YOU HAVE TO WRITE.)

AFTER YOU HAVE CREATED YOUR MINDMAP
REACH FOR A BLANK ONE
SAYING, "NOW LET'S DO ONE FOR YOU."

AS THEY WRITE THEIR NAME
IN THE SMALL MIDDLE OVAL
IN A VERY MATTER-OF-FACT TONE SAY:

"DO YOU WANT TO FILL IN THE LINES
OR DO YOU WANT ME TO?"

NEVER EMBARRASS OR INSULT YOUR LEARNING PARTNERS
BY PRESUMING IGNORANCE
>   OR DISINTEREST
OR BY TAKING OVER AND DOING SOMETHING
THEY MIGHT BE ABLE TO DO AS WELL, GIVEN THE CHOICE.

A B C D E F G H I J K L M N O P Q R S T U V W X Y Z

A
B
C
D
E
F
G
H
I
J
K
L
M
N
O
P
Q
R
S
T
U
V
W
X
Y
Z

THE BEAUTIES OF NATURE COME IN ALL COLORS.
THE STRENGTHS OF HUMANKIND COME IN MANY FORMS.
EVERY BEING IS WONDERFULLY UNIQUE.
ALL OF US CONTRIBUTE IN DIFFERENT WAYS.
WHEN WE LEARN TO HONOR THE DIFFERENCE
AND APPRECIATE THE MIX,
WE FIND HARMONY.
--ANONYMOUS

WHETHER THEY WRITE
OR YOU DO
GET THEM TO TALK.

TOGETHER
BUILD A WEB, A CLUSTER
AS THEY TELL THEIR TALE:

> WHERE THEY LIVE
> NAMES OF FAMILY MEMBERS
> NAMES OF THEIR FRIENDS
> SOME OF THEIR FAVORITE THINGS.

WHETHER YOU'RE WORKING WITH ADULTS
                                                    YOUTH
                                        CHILDREN
YOU MIGHT WANT TO BRING
SOME PENCIL CRAYONS OR CRAYOLAS.

INVITE THEM TO ADD COLOR
            TO THEIR NAME
            TO THE LINES.
PERHAPS THEY'LL WANT TO ADD
SOME STICK FIGURES
AND OTHER SIMPLE DRAWINGS.

DO LIKEWISE WITH YOUR MINDMAP.
YOU'LL BOTH FIND THAT
EVEN JUST A BIT OF COLOR
TRANSFORMS THE OUTCOME.

URGE THEM TO TAKE THEIR CREATIVE WORK HOME
AS A SOUVENIR OF THEIR FIRST SESSION
WITH YOU, THEIR NEW LEARNING PARTNER.

CHANCES ARE
THEY WILL BE THINKING, MAYBE EVEN SAYING

"HEY! THAT'S COOL.
AND IT'S ALL ABOUT ME!"

CHANCES ARE
THEY WILL ALSO BE LOOKING FORWARD TO THE NEXT SESSION.

A B C D E F G H I J K L M N O P Q R S T U V W X Y Z

A
B
C
D
E
F
G
H
I
J
K
L
M
N
O
P
Q
R
S
T
U
V
W
X
Y
Z

THE BIGGEST RULE OF IMPROV IS
YES, AND.
IF SOMEONE GIVES YOU AN OFFER,
YOU ACCEPT THAT OFFER
AND YOU BUILD ON THAT OFFER.
YOU HAVE TO LET GO OF YOUR AGENDA.
--WAYNE BRADY

32

<u>WHAT</u> DO YOU DO THE SECOND TIME YOU MEET?

WHEN YOU MEET AGAIN, AFTER YOU'RE COMFORTABLE
AND READY TO GET DOWN TO BUSINESS
YOU MIGHT DO A BRIEF **FOUR-LEVEL REFLECTION**
ON THE FIRST SESSION.
BE CASUAL. KEEP IT CONVERSATIONAL.
AND BE SURE TO INSERT SOME OF YOUR THOUGHTS TOO.

FACTS	WHAT DO YOU REMEMBER FROM THE FIRST SESSION? WHAT STRUCK YOU?
FEELINGS	OF EVERYTHING WE DID, WHAT DID YOU LIKE BEST? …LEAST? DID ANYTHING SURPRISE YOU?
LEARNINGS	IS ANYTHING CLEARER TO YOU NOW? WHAT DID YOU LEARN ABOUT YOURSELF?
NEEDS/NEXT	WHAT ARE YOU HOPING WE WILL REPEAT? …DO NEXT? …NOT DO?

THOSE ARE SOME OF THE QUESTIONS YOU CAN ASK.
VARY THEM.

YOU MAY FIND IT HELPFUL
TO USE THIS SIMPLE TOOL REGULARLY
AS A REVIEW AT THE BEGINNING OF EACH SESSION OR
AS A SUMMATION AT THE END.

BE SURE TO ASK FOR YOUR LEARNING PARTNERS' PERMISSION
TO TAKE NOTES DURING THAT CONVERSATION
SO THAT YOU'LL ALWAYS HAVE THEIR INPUT
AS YOU PLAN THE NEXT SESSION.

AND WHEN YOU FOLLOW THEIR SUGGESTIONS
LET THEM KNOW THAT THEY ARE RIGHT ON TARGET.

TELL THEM THAT YOU VALUE THEIR ONGOING FEEDBACK
AND ALL THE IDEAS THEY CAN COME UP WITH.

BUILD A REAL LEARNING PARTNERSHIP.

A B C D E F G H I J K L M N O P Q R S T U V W X Y Z

A
B
C
D
E
F
G
H
I
J
K
L
M
N
O
P
Q
R
S
T
U
V
W
X
Y
Z

COMPASSION
IS THE KEEN AWARENESS
OF THE INTERDEPENDENCE
OF ALL THINGS.
--*THOMAS MERTON*

PRECISELY BECAUSE YOU ARE PARTNERS IN THIS ENDEAVOR
YOU MAY WANT TO LIMIT THE USE OF THE TITLE TUTOR
AND AVOID USING THAT STRANGE, DISTANCING WORD, TUTEE.

WHATEVER YOUR RESPECTIVE AGES
YOU EACH BRING SOMETHING UNIQUE TO THE TABLE
IN A DIALOGUE OF EQUALS.

AS YOU WILL DISCOVER MORE AND MORE
YOU ARE INDEED
LEARNING FROM EACH OTHER.

NOW, JUST AS THE FIRST MINDMAP
WAS MEANT TO HELP YOU AND YOUR LEARNING PARTNER
GET TO KNOW EACH OTHER A BIT
HERE'S AN OPTION FOR THE SECOND SESSION.

THE DELIGHTFUL **JUDITH VIORST** PIECE
THAT FOLLOWS
WILL GIVE YOU ANOTHER GLIMPSE
AT YOUR LEARNING PARTNER'S LIFE
A PEEK AT SOME OF THE FEARS
                    FRUSTRATIONS
                    FANTASIES
OF THE UNIQUE INDIVIDUAL
WHO HAS CHOSEN TO WORK WITH YOU.

THE FOCUS OF THIS POEM
IS JUDITH VIORST'S SON:
A KID WHO WISHES HE WERE
IN CHARGE OF THE WORLD…
AS WE ALL DO
AT ONE TIME OR ANOTHER.

AND A SIMPLE MINDMAP
THAT YOU CONSTRUCT TOGETHER
WILL GIVE YOUR LEARNING PARTNERS
WORDS WITH WHICH TO CREATE
THEIR OWN POEM—
A POEM THEY WILL TAKE HOME TO KEEP
A POEM THAT WILL BECOME A CONFIDENCE-BUILDING MEMORY
OF THIS NEW LEARNING ADVENTURE
THAT THEY HAVE BEGUN WITH YOU.

ABCDEFGHIJKLMNOPQRSTUVWXYZ

A
B
C
D
E
F
G
H
I
J
K
L
M
N
O
P
Q
R
S
T
U
V
W
X
Y
Z

ONLY CONNECT...
--*E. M. FORSTER*

IF I WERE IN CHARGE OF THE WORLD
BY JUDITH VIORST

IF I WERE IN CHARGE OF THE WORLD
I'D CANCEL OATMEAL,
MONDAY MORNINGS,
ALLERGY SHOTS, AND ALSO
SARA STEINBERG.

IF I WERE IN CHARGE OF THE WORLD
THERE'D BE BRIGHTER NIGHT LIGHTS,
HEALTHIER HAMSTERS, AND
BASKETBALL BASKETS FORTY-EIGHT INCHES LOWER.

IF I WERE IN CHARGE OF THE WORLD
YOU WOULDN'T HAVE LONELY.
YOU WOULDN'T HAVE CLEAN.
YOU WOULDN'T HAVE BEDTIMES.
OR "DON'T PUNCH YOUR SISTER."
YOU WOULDN'T EVEN HAVE SISTERS.

IF I WERE IN CHARGE OF THE WORLD
A CHOCOLATE SUNDAE WITH WHIPPED CREAM AND NUTS
     WOULD BE A VEGETABLE.
ALL 007 MOVIES WOULD BE G.
AND A PERSON WHO SOMETIMES FORGOT TO BRUSH,
AND SOMETIMES FORGOT TO FLUSH,
WOULD STILL BE ALLOWED TO BE
IN CHARGE OF THE WORLD.

A B C D E F G H I J K L M N O P Q R S T U V W X Y Z

A
B
C
D
E
F
G
H
I
J
K
L
M
N
O
P
Q
R
S
T
U
V
W
X
Y
Z

EVERY ADULT
NEEDS A CHILD TO TEACH;
IT'S THE WAY ADULTS LEARN.
--WAYNE SANSTEAD

AFTER YOU HAVE READ THE POEM ALOUD ONCE OR TWICE
SHARE WITH YOUR LEARNING PARTNER A BRIEF ANECDOTE
TIED INTO A LINE WITH WHICH YOU IDENTIFY.

IN CONCRETE TERMS, AS JUDITH VIORST DOES
VERY BRIEFLY TALK ABOUT A FEW OF YOUR OWN SIMPLE
FEARS, FRUSTRATIONS, AND FANTASIES.

"IF I WERE IN CHARGE OF THE WORLD
I'D CANCEL …"

AND

"THERE'D BE…"

AND

"YOU WOULDN'T HAVE…"

THEN, ENCOURAGE YOUR LEARNING PARTNERS TO DO LIKEWISE.
AND AS THEY BEGIN
TELL THEM THAT YOU WOULD LIKE TO PUT THEIR WORDS
ON THE MINDMAP BEFORE YOU
AND SEE WHERE IT LEADS THEM.

USING THE PROMPTS ABOVE
AND A COPY OF THE MINDMAP IN THE BACK OF THIS BOOK
CREATE A WEB WITH THEIR VERY OWN WORDS.

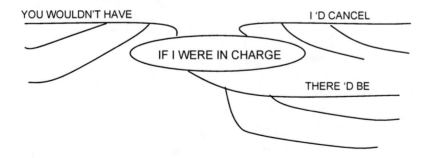

YOU WOULDN'T HAVE   I 'D CANCEL

IF I WERE IN CHARGE

THERE 'D BE

A B C D E F G H I J K L M N O P Q R S T U V W X Y Z

A
B
C
D
E
F
G
H
I
J
K
L
M
N
O
P
Q
R
S
T
U
V
W
X
Y
Z

WE COME TO KNOW OURSELVES
BY OUR RESISTANCES.
--CHARLES OLSON

WHEN THEY ARE READY TO STOP
ASK THEM
IF THEY WOULD LIKE TO TURN *THEIR* WORDS
INTO A POEM LIKE JUDITH VIORST'S.

THE FRAGMENT BELOW
IS A SAMPLE OF HOW TO GET STARTED.

AGAIN, ASK THEM
IF THEY WANT TO WRITE IT THEMSELVES
OR IF THEY WANT YOU
TO DO THE WRITING.

YOU MAY VERY WELL RAISE INTEREST
BY NOT PRESUMING DISINTEREST
AND A VISION OF POSSIBILITY
BY NOT IMPOSING LIMITS
OR A FOREGONE CONCLUSION.

IF I WERE IN CHARGE
BY *IMA POET*

(WITH A TIP OF THE HAT TO JUDITH VIORST)

IF I WERE IN CHARGE OF THE WORLD
I'D CANCEL QUIZZES,
…

IF I WERE IN CHARGE OF THE WORLD
THERE'D BE LONGER SUMMERS,
…

IF I WERE IN CHARGE OF THE WORLD
YOU WOULDN'T HAVE SCARED,
…

A B C D E F G H I J K L M N O P Q R S T U V W X Y Z

A
B
C
D
E
F
G
H
I
J
K
L
M
N
O
P
Q
R
S
T
U
V
W
X
Y
Z

THE LIMIT WAS IN THEIR MINDS.
IT REPRESENTED THE RANGE OF ENERGY
THEY WOULD ALLOW THEMSELVES
TO EXPERIENCE.
--*RICHARD MOSS*

AS YOU AND YOUR LEARNING PARTNERS
READ THE WORDS ON THEIR MINDMAP
LET THEM CHOOSE THE THOUGHTS
THAT THEY WISH TO INCORPORATE
INTO THEIR POEM.

WHAT THEY CREATE
CAN BE LONGER
OR SHORTER
THAN JUDITH VIORST'S CREATION.
IT IS THEIRS!

IF THEY TEND TO FOCUS
ON LOOKING FOR RHYMING WORDS
HELP THEM TO NOTICE THAT
WITH THE EXCEPTION OF BRUSH AND FLUSH
IN THE LAST STANZA
JUDITH VIORST'S POEM
IS BLANK VERSE.
LIKE SHAKESPEARE'S PLAYS!

HAVE FUN WITH WHAT WILL PROBABLY BE
A WHOLE NEW EXPERIENCE
AND CREATIVE EXPERIMENT.

ONCE THE POEM SUITS THEM
THERE MAY BE A COMPUTER NEARBY
IN THE PUBLIC SPACE WHERE YOU MEET.
OR THEY SIMPLY MAY WANT TO REWRITE IT.

WHATEVER THE END PRODUCT
URGE THEM TO TAKE IT WITH THEM
TO READ TO FRIENDS AND FAMILY
IF THEY SO CHOOSE.

BE SURE TO **KEEP A COPY FOR THEIR FILE**
SO THAT YOU CAN READ IT TOGETHER AGAIN
AT THEIR NEXT SESSION.

THAT WILL ALSO ALLOW YOU TO MAKE COPIES
IF THEY WANT TO SHARE THEIR POEM WITH OTHERS
DOWN THE ROAD.

A B C D E F G H I J K L M N O P Q R S T U V W X Y Z

A
B
C
D
E
F
G
H
I
J
K
L
M
N
O
P
Q
R
S
T
U
V
W
X
Y
Z

IT IS ONLY WITH THE HEART
THAT WE CAN SEE CLEARLY.
WHAT IS ESSENTIAL
IS INVISIBLE TO THE EYES.
--*ANTOINE DE SAINT-EXUPÉRY*

HOW DO YOU ACCELERATE LEARNING?

HOW **DO** YOU ACCELERATE LEARNING?

ASK **QUESTIONS**.
LISTEN.

LET YOUR LEARNING PARTNERS **TALK**.
LISTEN.

NOTICE THE **WORDS**.
LISTEN.

LOOK FOR **CLUES**.
LISTEN.

WATCH THEIR **EYES**.
LISTEN.

FIND THEIR **INTERESTS**.
LISTEN.

FIND THEIR **PASSION**.
LISTEN.

LISTEN
WITH YOUR **EARS**.

LISTEN
WITH YOUR **EYES**.

LISTEN
WITH YOUR **HEART**.

45

A B C D E F G H I J K L M N O P Q R S T U V W X Y Z

A
B
C
D
E
F
G
H
I
J
K
L
M
N
O
P
Q
R
S
T
U
V
W
X
Y
Z

ORGANIC READING FOR BEGINNERS
IS NOT NEW;
IT'S OUR REJECTION OF IT
THAT'S NEW
--SYLVIA ASHTON-WARNER

46

WHETHER YOUR LEARNING PARTNERS ARE HESITANT READERS
OR DO NOT READ AT ALL
ASK QUESTIONS:

> QUESTIONS THAT WILL FIRE THEM UP;
> QUESTIONS ABOUT INTERESTS
> THEY HAVE ALREADY SPOKEN OF
> > IN THE MINDMAPS
> > IN THE POETRY
> > IN CONVERSATIONS WITH YOU.

AS THEY TALK AND AS YOU DIALOGUE
JOT DOWN **KEY WORDS**, IMPORTANT WORDS
WORDS THAT ARE AN INTEGRAL PART
OF THE WORLD OF WHICH THEY SPEAK.

WHEN THEY COME UP FOR AIR
TURN A FILE CARD TOWARD THEM
AND ON IT, IN LARGE CAPS
PRINT THE MOST IMPORTANT OF THOSE KEY WORDS.

"THIS IS WHAT YOU'RE TALKING ABOUT!"
SAY IT ENTHUSIASTICALLY.

MOST LIKELY, THEY WILL BE ABLE TO READ IT
BECAUSE IT SUMS UP
SOMETHING OF IMPORTANCE
TO THEM.

AS SYLVIA ASHTON-WARNER LEARNED
WHEN SHE TAUGHT MAORI PRE-SCHOOLERS TO READ
THAT WORD MAY BE A
> **ONE-LOOK WORD**
PART OF THE NEW READER'S
> **ORGANIC, KEY VOCABULARY**.

WORDS FROM THE GUT, WHICH WE CALL
> **SIGHT WORDS**
MAY ALLOW YOU TO BUILD
> **RHYMING WORD LISTS**
THAT WILL GREATLY ACCELERATE
THE DECODING PROCESS, THE TEACHING OF PHONICS.

A B C D E F G H I J K L M N O P Q R S T U V W X Y Z

A
B
C
D
E
F
G
H
I
J
K
L
M
N
O
P
Q
R
S
T
U
V
W
X
Y
Z

EDUCATION IS NOT
THE FILLING OF A BUCKET,
BUT THE LIGHTING OF A FIRE.
--*WILLIAM BUTLER YEATS*

INVITE YOUR LEARNING PARTNERS
TO TELL YOU STORIES
ANECDOTES FROM THEIR DAILY LIFE.

THE MORE MEANINGFUL THE STORY IS TO THEM
THE MORE IT STILL HAS RELEVANCE
THE MORE POWERFUL THE TELLING WILL BE.

ASK THEIR PERMISSION TO WRITE DOWN
WHAT THEY SAY, AS THEY SAY IT.
AVOID THE TEMPTATION TO CONTINUALLY CORRECT THEM.

ON LINED PAPER (PREFERABLY)
WRITE VERY LEGIBLE CAPITAL LETTERS AS THEY SPEAK.
AS IN THIS BOOK, START A NEW LINE FREQUENTLY
SO THAT WHOLE PHRASES HANG TOGETHER
AND LONG SENTENCES ARE BROKEN INTO COHERENT PARTS.
DON'T BE AFRAID TO USE A LOT OF PAPER.
TELL THEM THAT WHAT YOU WRITE WILL BE THEIRS TO KEEP.

TOPICS THAT MAY GET THEM GOING :
       BEST FRIEND, FAVORITE RELATIVE, BELOVED PET…
       FIRST JOB, FIRST DAY IN SCHOOL, IN TRAINING…
       FAVORITE (OR WORST) BOSS, TEACHER, COACH…
       A BIG SURPRISE, SCARE, RESPONSIBILITY…
       SPECIAL HOLIDAYS, HOLY DAYS, BIRTHDAYS…
       LEARNING TO SWIM, DRIVE A CAR, PLAY SOCCER…

ONCE THEY GET GOING, WAIT UNTIL THEY ARE READY TO STOP.
THEN, ASK THEM IF THEY WOULD LIKE TO READ
WHAT YOU WROTE DOWN AS THEY SPOKE.

HOWEVER LONG THEIR STORY IS, IF IT CAME FROM THE HEART
EVEN NEW READERS MAY BE ABLE TO READ MOST, IF NOT ALL OF IT.
YOU WILL BE SURPRISED; AND SO WILL THEY.

JUST WATCH THEIR CONFIDENCE GROW
AS YOU REPEAT THIS ACTIVITY AND BUILD ON THE SIGHT WORDS
THAT COME TUMBLING OUT OF THEIR MOUTH
WITH LITTLE OR NO PRODDING FROM YOU.

THAT IS THE POWER OF THE **LANGUAGE EXPERIENCE APPROACH**.
WHAT COMES FROM THE HEART IS REAL.
THEY OWN IT. IT IS THEIRS.

A B C D E F G H I J K L M N O P Q R S T U V W X Y Z

A
B
C
D
E
F
G
H
I
J
K
L
M
N
O
P
Q
R
S
T
U
V
W
X
Y
Z

A SEED HIDDEN
IN THE HEART OF AN APPLE
IS AN ORCHARD INVISIBLE.
--WELSH PROVERB

HOWEVER, ALTHOUGH ENGLISH IS RELATIVELY EASY
TO LEARN TO SPEAK
ENGLISH SPELLING IS NOTORIOUSLY STRANGE
COMPARED TO OTHER LANGUAGES.

LIKE MAGPIES
WE ENGLISH SPEAKERS
HAVE ENRICHED OUR VOCABULARY OVER THE CENTURIES
BY GARNERING WORDS FROM COUNTLESS OTHER LANGUAGES
AND MAKING THEM OUR OWN.

NOW, BACK TO THE WORD—
THE WORD THAT YOU WROTE IN BIG LETTERS ON A FILE CARD
THE KEY WORD FROM YOUR LEARNING PARTNER'S CONVERSATION.

IF THAT KEY WORD IS SPELLED PHONETICALLY
AND THEY STILL CAN'T READ IT
      SAY IT ALOUD
      AND HAVE THEM REPEAT IT.

PRECISELY BECAUSE IT'S AN IMPORTANT WORD TO THEM
AFTER YOU HAVE SAID IT ALOUD
IT MAY INDEED BECOME
         A ONE-LOOK WORD
         A SIGHT WORD.

IF NOT, YOU MAY DECIDE
TO **DECODE** IT WITH THEM.

WHAT BETTER WAY TO **INTRODUCE PHONICS**
THAN WITH A SELF-CHOSEN WORD
THAT MEANS SOMETHING SPECIAL TO THEM?

UNTIL YOUR LEARNING PARTNERS
GET USED TO BLENDING THE LETTERS
THIS IS **THE SIMPLEST WAY TO DECODE A WORD**:

1-   BREAK EACH SYL - LA - BLE
        INTO SOUND SEGMENTS…
2-   THEN LINK A SERIES OF TWO SOUND SEGMENTS…
        AS YOU SLOWLY BUILD THE WORD WITH THEM.

LET'S SEE HOW TO DO THAT.

A B C D E F G H I J K L M N O P Q R S T U V W X Y Z

A
B
C
D
E
F
G
H
I
J
K
L
M
N
O
P
Q
R
S
T
U
V
W
X
Y
Z

DO THE THING
AND YOU SHALL HAVE THE POWER.
SKILL TO DO COMES OF DOING.
--RALPH WALDO EMERSON

To illustrate, let's use the word **DOG**
which has 1 syllable,
3 letters
5 sound segments.

Say **D** (sound segment #1) in isolation
with virtually no vowel sound:
(Do not say a clunky Duh;
more like a soft Dih.)   **/D/**

Then say the next sound segment (#2)
in isolation
pronouncing it
as in the word *ON*:   **O**

Put those two initial sound segments
together into one sound segment (#3)
that rhymes with *LAW*:   **DO..**

Say the hard **G** lightly
(sound segment #4):   **/G/**

Then add it
to the previous sound segment (#3):   **DO..G**

And you have sound segment #5: the word   **DOG**

This illustration looks complicated on paper.

It is not, however
if you **BEGIN WITH SIMPLE PHONETIC WORDS.**

Once your Learning Partners get used to blending
two consecutive sound segments at a time
they will need to do it
less and less frequently.

They will soon be on their way
to becoming
independent readers.

A B C D E F G H I J K L M N O P Q R S T U V W X Y Z

A
B
C
D
E
F
G
H
I
J
K
L
M
N
O
P
Q
R
S
T
U
V
W
X
Y
Z

A BOOK SHOULD SERVE AS AN AX
FOR THE FROZEN SEA
WITHIN US.
--*FRANZ KAFKA*

<u>WHY</u> ARE SOME DIFFICULT BOOKS EASIER TO READ?

BRING BOOKS:
>
> YOUR OWN BOOKS
> LIBRARY BOOKS
> USED BOOKS.

BRING BOOKS THAT FEED THE INTERESTS
OF YOUR LEARNING PARTNERS
AND BOOKS THAT MAY BE OFFSHOOTS OF THOSE INTERESTS.

BRING BOOKS THAT WILL STRETCH THEM
IF THEY SEEM READY TO BE STRETCHED.

IF YOU HAVE MISREAD THEM
AND THEY SHOW NO REAL INTEREST
MOVE ON TO SOMETHING ELSE.

IF YOU ARE NOT MEETING AT A LIBRARY
ENCOURAGE THEM
>
> TO VISIT THEIR LOCAL LIBRARY
> TO GET A LIBRARY CARD AND
> TO USE IT REGULARLY.

ENGAGE THE READERS
AND THEIR FAMILIES
IN THE SEARCH FOR MEANINGFUL BOOKS AND MAGAZINES.

DEPENDING ON THEIR AGE AND EXPERIENCE
THEY MAY BE INTERESTED IN
>
> DOGS OR CATS OR DINOSAURS.

THEY MAY HAVE A PASSION FOR
>
> CARS OR BASKETBALL
> COOKING OR FASHION
> THE SACRED SCRIPTURE OF THEIR RELIGION.

OR PERHAPS THEY WANT TO LEARN
EVERYTHING THEY CAN ABOUT
>
> PREGNANCY, PARENTHOOD
> AND CARING FOR A NEWBORN.

A B C D E F G H I J K L M N O P Q R S T U V W X Y Z

A
B
C
D
E
F
G
H
I
J
K
L
M
N
O
P
Q
R
S
T
U
V
W
X
Y
Z

EXPERIENCE IS NOT WHAT HAPPENS TO YOU.
IT IS WHAT YOU DO
WITH WHAT HAPPENS TO YOU.
--ALDOUS HUXLEY

ENCOURAGE AND SUPPORT WITH ENTHUSIASM
WHATEVER INTERESTS YOUR LEARNING PARTNERS HAVE .

WITH MUCH LESS EFFORT AND NO DRUDGERY
THOSE INTERESTS MAY BECOME
          LAUNCHING PADS TO READING ACCELERATION
          SPRINGBOARDS TO SUCCESS.

THE JUVENILE AND CHILDREN'S SECTIONS
OF BOOKSTORES AND LIBRARIES
ARE GOOD PLACES TO FIND EASY-TO-READ BOOKS
ABOUT COMPLEX THINGS.

OLDER HESITANT READERS DO NOT MIND READING EASY BOOKS
ABOUT THINGS IN WHICH THEY ARE DEEPLY INTERESTED.

THE REASON IS CRUCIAL:
THEY ALREADY HAVE AN INTERNAL VOCABULARY
WHICH THE EASY BOOKS WILL HELP THEM
TO RECOGNIZE FROM CONTEXT.

CHOOSE BOOKS THAT ARE A SLIGHT STRETCH
          BOOKS THAT HAVE LOTS OF REPETITIONS
          BOOKS WITH SILLY RHYMES
LIKE DR. SEUSS'S *THERE'S A WOCKET IN MY POCKET.* *

JUDITH VIORST'S *ALEXANDER AND THE TERRIBLE, HORRIBLE,*
                    NO GOOD, VERY BAD DAY
IS ANOTHER GREAT BOOK FOR KIDS AND EVEN ADULTS.
HESITANT READERS MAY BEGIN TO REBUILD SELF-CONFIDENCE
IF, AS YOU READ ALOUD, YOU HAVE THEM LOOK AHEAD
FOR THE MANY ITERATIONS OF THAT WONDERFUL CHORUS:

          "TERRIBLE, HORRIBLE, NO GOOD, VERY BAD DAY."

DEPENDING ON THEIR SKILL
YOU MAY HAVE TO READ EVERYTHING ELSE IN THAT BOOK;
BUT YOU WILL BOTH HAVE FUN IN THE PROCESS.

* THERE ARE ONLY 50 DIFFERENT WORDS IN *GREEN EGGS AND HAM. THE CAT IN THE HAT*
  CONTAINS 225 OF THE WORDS THAT FIRST GRADERS OF 1957 NEEDED TO LEARN. BOTH
  WERE WRITTEN ON A DARE FROM DR. SEUSS'S PUBLISHER.

A B C D E F G H I J K L M N O P Q R S T U V W X Y Z

A
B
C
D
E
F
G
H
I
J
K
L
M
N
O
P
Q
R
S
T
U
V
W
X
Y
Z

ARE YOU SINGING AS YOU HAVE SUNG, EARTHMILES AWAY?
... UNBANDAGE THESE EYES, UNBIND THESE FEET.
--NELLIE WONG

58

INTRODUCE YOUR LEARNING PARTNERS
TO THE BOOKS OF FAMILY-FOCUSED HUMORISTS
LIKE ERMA BOMBECK
AND BILL COSBY.

READ THE SPORTS PAGE WITH THEM
SONG LYRICS
JOKE BOOKS
MAGAZINES
CARTOONS.

(HAVE YOU EVER NOTICED
THAT CARTOON DIALOGUE IS PRINTED IN SMALL CAPS
LIKE THIS BOOK? MORE ON THAT LATER.)

TAKE TIME
TO GET AN OVERVIEW OF THE MATERIAL:
THE TITLE OF A BOOK
THE AUTHOR
THE ILLUSTRATOR.
IF THERE ARE NO PICTURES
YOU MAY WANT TO READ
SOME OF THE CHAPTER TITLES ALOUD.

IF YOUR LEARNING PARTNERS KNOW THE BASICS
INVITE THEM TO READ
UNTIL THEY WANT YOU TO TAKE OVER.

OR THEY MAY WANT YOU TO START.
HAVE FUN ALTERNATING.

WHATEVER THEIR PROFICIENCY
FROM NEW READERS
TO THOSE WHO SIMPLY WISH TO IMPROVE THEIR SKILLS

FIND SOMETHING
BEYOND THEIR OWN READ-ALOUD SKILL LEVEL
AND
REGULARLY READ ALOUD TO THEM A BIT:
A FUNNY SEGMENT
A BRIEF CHAPTER
AN ENGROSSING SERIAL.

WHET THEIR APPETITE FOR MORE.

A B C D E F G H I J K L M N O P Q R S T U V W X Y Z

A
B
C
D
E
F
G
H
I
J
K
L
M
N
O
P
Q
R
S
T
U
V
W
X
Y
Z

THE WORLD OF BOOKS
IS THE MOST REMARKABLE CREATION OF MAN.
NOTHING ELSE THAT HE BUILDS EVER LASTS.
MONUMENTS FALL, NATIONS PERISH...
BUT IN THE WORLD OF BOOKS
ARE VOLUMES THAT LIVE ON,
STILL AS YOUNG AND FRESH AS THE DAY THEY WERE WRITTEN,
STILL TELLING MEN'S HEARTS
OF THE HEARTS OF MEN CENTURIES DEAD.
--CLARENCE DAY

60

YOUNG AND OLD
HELP THEM CREATE A LIST
OF MOVIES THEY LIKE.
ADD TO IT AS THEY THINK OF OTHERS.

SOME OF THEIR FAVORITES
MAY HAVE BEEN MADE
FROM NOVELS
FROM CHILDREN'S BOOKS
FROM BOOKS THAT YOU OR THEY
MAY HAVE AT HOME
OR THAT YOU CAN BORROW FROM THE LIBRARY.

READ INTERESTING SECTIONS OF THE ORIGINAL.

READ FROM BIOGRAPHIES
SHORT STORIES
HOW-TO BOOKS
FAIRY TALES
MYSTERIES
POETRY.

THE POSSIBILITIES ARE ENDLESS.

SIT NEXT TO THE READER
OR TOGETHER
AT THE CORNER OF A TABLE.

WHETHER YOUR LEARNING PARTNERS
READ SILENTLY OR ALOUD
DEPENDS ON THEIR PREFERENCE
AND THEIR PROFICIENCY.

NEW READERS
WILL NEED TO SPEND MORE TIME
READING ALOUD.

BUT...
DROP
WHATEVER
BORES THEM
AND CHOOSE SOMETHING ELSE.

A B C D E F G H I J K L M N O P Q R S T U V W X Y Z

A
B
C
D
E
F
G
H
I
J
K
L
M
N
O
P
Q
R
S
T
U
V
W
X
Y
Z

MAN WHO SAYS IT CANNOT BE DONE
SHOULD NOT INTERRUPT
MAN WHO IS DOING IT.
--*CHINESE PROVERB*

<u>HOW</u> DO YOU TEACH PHONICS IN CONTEXT?

IF YOUR LEARNING PARTNERS PREFER TO READ SILENTLY
EACH TIME THEY COME TO UNFAMILIAR WORDS
ENCOURAGE THEM TO POINT TO THOSE WORDS.
AND WHEN THEY DO

IMMEDIATELY **GIVE THEM THE WORDS**.

IF THEY ARE READING ALOUD
WHENEVER THEY HESITATE

IMMEDIATELY AND QUIETLY, **GIVE THEM THE WORDS**.

GIVE THEM THE WORDS, AND LET THEM MOVE ON.

AND IF THEY USE A SYNONYM (FOR EXAMPLE, DOOR FOR GATE)
DO **NOT** CORRECT THEM.
THEY HAVE THE MEANING RIGHT.
YOUR RESTRAINT WILL ENABLE THEM TO BEGIN TO EXPERIENCE
WHAT READING IS ALL ABOUT:
             MAKING SENSE OUT OF WORDS STRUNG TOGETHER
             GETTING CAUGHT UP IN THE STORY
             WANTING TO KNOW WHAT HAPPENS NEXT.

YES, THEY MUST LEARN TO DECODE
OR THEY WILL NEVER BECOME INDEPENDENT READERS.

      BUT DO
NOT INTERRUPT THE
      FLOW OF THE
STORY TO TEACH PHONICS.

TEACH PHONICS
WHEN THEY COME TO A NATURAL STOPPING POINT
A POINT AT WHICH THEY WANT TO STOP.

AND SO THAT YOU WILL REMEMBER THE WORDS THEY DON'T KNOW
UNOBTRUSIVELY **LIST THE EASIEST OF THOSE WORDS**
FOR DECODING PRACTICE JUST AROUND THE CORNER.

THE VERY WORDS YOU HAVE GIVEN THEM
WILL BE GRIST FOR THE PHONICS MILL.

A B C D E F G H I J K L M N O P Q R S T U V W X Y Z

A
B
C
D
E
F
G
H
I
J
K
L
M
N
O
P
Q
R
S
T
U
V
W
X
Y
Z

IT'S WHAT WE LEARN
AFTER WE THINK WE KNOW IT ALL
THAT COUNTS.
--KIM L. HUBBARD

WHEN YOUR LEARNING PARTNERS FINISH
WHATEVER THEY ARE CAUGHT UP IN—
    A SENTENCE
    A PARAGRAPH
    A PAGE—
WHEN THEY HAVE READ ENOUGH TO SATISFY THEMSELVES
TOGETHER YOU WILL BEGIN TO CREATE
A RHYMING WORD BOOK OR, IF THEY PREFER, A DECK OF RHYMES.

FROM THE BACK OF THIS BOOK
CUT A STRIP LIKE THE ONE AT THE TOP OF THE FACING PAGE
OR MAKE YOUR OWN BY HAND OR ON YOUR COMPUTER.

    NOTICE THAT THE VOWELS—A, E, I, O, U—ARE SMALLER.
    THEREFORE, TO EMPHASIZE THEIR IMPORTANCE
    YOU MIGHT INVITE YOUR LEARNING PARTNER
    TO COLOR THOSE FIVE VOWELS * ON THE ALPHABET STRIP
    WITH A SOFT HIGHLIGHTER.
    WHY? SO THAT THE VOWELS WILL NOT GET LOST IN THE SHUFFLE
    WHEN YOU GO THROUGH THE ALPHABET
    FOCUSED ON INITIAL CONSONANT SOUNDS
    AS YOU LOOK FOR RHYMING WORDS.

PLACE THE ALPHABET STRIP ABOVE A FILE CARD
    OR ABOVE A BLANK PAGE IN A SMALL NOTEBOOK. **
THEN TAKE THE SIMPLEST AND EASIEST WORD
FROM THE LIST YOU DISCREETLY MADE
WHEN YOUR LEARNING PARTNER STUMBLED
AND **CREATE A WORD LIST**
    A LIST OF RHYMING WORDS
THAT WILL ANCHOR THAT PARTICULAR WORD
AND MANY OTHERS LIKE IT IN YOUR LEARNING PARTNER'S MIND.

BE SURE TO **PRINT PLAIN CAPITAL LETTERS**
TO AVOID LOWERCASE REVERSALS THAT MAY BEDEVIL NEW READERS WHO DON'T
YET SEE THE DIFFERENCE BETWEEN **b d p q**.

---

* THE SIXTH VOWEL ("…AND SOMETIMES Y") SOUNDS LIKE E OR I AND IS USUALLY WITHIN
  OR AT THE END OF A WORD, AS IN SILLY, STORY, AND SYLLABLE.
  AS A CONSONANT, Y IS MOST OFTEN AT THE BEGINNING OF A WORD, AS IN YES, YOU, AND
  YIPPEE.
**SEE THE ILLUSTRATIONS IN THE NEXT SECTION, AND LEARN HOW TO TEACH PHONICS BY
  BUILDING LISTS OF RHYMING WORDS.

A B C D E F G H I J K L M N O P Q R S T U V W X Y Z

A
B
C
D
E
F
G
H
I
J
K
L
M
N
O
P
Q
R
S
T
U
V
W
X
Y
Z

DISCOVERY IS SEEING
WHAT EVERYBODY ELSE HAS SEEN
AND THINKING
WHAT NOBODY ELSE HAS THOUGHT.
--ALBERT SZENT-GYORGI

<u>WHY</u> USE UPPERCASE LETTERS TO TEACH DECODING?

IF YOU HAD NEVER CRACKED THE CODE
IF THE SYMBOLS OF THE ALPHABET WERE GREEK TO YOU
THEN YOU WOULD FIND
THAT IT IS MUCH EASIER TO READ   **B D P Q**
        than it is to read   **b d p q**

WHY ON EARTH IS THAT?
DR. RENÉE FULLER * EXPLAINS IT THUS:

B D P ARE EASIER TO READ THAN **b d p**
BECAUSE, WHEN THERE IS A **VERTICAL LINE**
IT IS ALWAYS **ON THE LEFT** OF AN UPPERCASE LETTER
AND ALWAYS **ABOVE THE LINE**:   I B
                                     I D
                                     I P

With the lowercase letters, a **line**
attached to a little **circle** can be

left of the circle	**b**	**p**
or right of the circle	**d**	**q**
left or right above the line	**b**	**d**
left or right below the line	**p**	**q**

DO YOU SEE HOW CONFUSING THAT MAY BE FOR A NEW READER?

---

* THE FIRST EIGHT OF DR. FULLER'S TEN STORYBOOKS ARE PRINTED IN CAPITALS. IN HER SEMINAL RESEARCH, FULLER'S MULTI-SENSORY SYSTEM OF CAPITAL LETTERS ENABLED 24 OF 26 INSTITUTIONALIZED ADULTS AND YOUTH (WHOSE IQS RANGED FROM THE 33 TO 72) TO LEARN TO READ WITH ENTHUSIASM AND UNDERSTANDING. SOME TAUGHT THEMSELVES TO WRITE. OF THE 20 WHO HAD A POSITIVE CHANGE IN THEIR SOCIAL OR WORK CONDITIONS, FIVE WERE DISCHARGED. FULLER'S WORK HAS BEEN REPLICATED WITH INDIVIDUALS WITH IQS IN THE 20S. FORMERLY A STRONG BELIEVER IN THE IQ CORRELATION, HER RESEARCH NOW FOCUSES ON THE RELATIONSHIP OF WHAT SHE CALLS THE STORY ENGRAM TO THE GROWTH AND TRANSFORMATION OF REAL WORLD INTELLIGENCE. SEE *IN SEARCH OF THE IQ CORRELATION*, THE EXPANDED VERSION OF FULLER'S INITIAL AMERICAN PSYCHOLOGICAL ASSOCIATION SYMPOSIUM ON THE BALL-STICK-BIRD READING SYSTEM.

A B C D E F G H I J K L M N O P Q R S T U V W X Y Z

A
B
C
D
E
F
G
H
I
J
K
L
M
N
O
P
Q
R
S
T
U
V
W
X
Y
Z

INSANITY:
DOING THE SAME THINGS
OVER AND OVER AGAIN
AND EXPECTING DIFFERENT RESULTS.
--ANONYMOUS

To understand lowercase reversals better

TAKE AN OBJECT ON YOUR DESK: A STAPLER, FOR EXAMPLE.

IF YOU HOLD A STAPLER RIGHT SIDE UP, IT IS OBVIOUSLY A STAPLER.

HOLD IT UPSIDE DOWN, AND IT IS STILL A STAPLER.

PLACE IT ON ITS SIDE; IT IS STILL A STAPLER.

> NOT SO FOR **THE LINE AND THE CIRCLE** THAT MAKE UP
> LOWERCASE LETTERS LIKE **b d p q**.

THE PLACEMENT OF THE LINE AND THE CIRCLE
DETERMINES THE NAME OF THE LETTER THEY REPRESENT
WHICH IN TURN DETERMINES
THE RANGE OF SOUNDS THAT THE LETTER SYMBOL REPRESENTS.

YOU MAY SIT YOUR STAPLER ON THE DESK TO STAPLE PAPERS
OR HOLD IT VERTICALLY
TO STAPLE A NOTICE ON A BULLETIN BOARD.

NO MATTER HOW YOU HOLD IT, IT'S STILL A STAPLER.

The lowercase albhapet—oops—alphabet
does not work that way.
The lowercase patterns are not interchangeable.

> The **b**uick **d**rown fox jum**qep** over the lazy **god**.
> IS NOT THE SAME AS
> The **q**uick **b**rown fox jum**ped** over the lazy **dog**.

HOWEVER, THERE IS NO CONFUSION IF YOU USE CAPITAL LETTERS. *

> THE **Q**UICK **B**ROWN FOX JUM**P**ED OVER THE LAZY **D**OG.

THERE IS GREATER DIFFERENTIATION BETWEEN
THE **Q** OF QUICK AND THE **B** OF BROWN
THE **P** AND **D** OF JUMPED AND THE **D** AND **G** OF DOG.

THERE ARE FEWER OPPORTUNITIES TO MISREAD THE LETTERS
AND THEREFORE THERE IS LESS CONFUSION.

---

* ALWAYS USE PLAIN CAPITALS WITH NO SERIFS, **NO LITTLE LINES THAT MAY CONFUSE THE HESITANT READER.**

A B C D E F G H I J K L M N O P Q R S T U V W X Y Z

A
B
C
D
E
F
G
H
I
J
K
L
M
N
O
P
Q
R
S
T
U
V
W
X
Y
Z

THE SECRET OF
WALKING ON WATER
IS KNOWING
WHERE THE STONES ARE.
--*HERB COHEN*

70

IF NEW READERS CANNOT READ THE WORD
IT'S BECAUSE THE WORD IS UNFAMILIAR OR NOT REMEMBERED
OR THEY HAVE NO RHYMING WORD—YET—TO HANG IT ON.
BUT PROBABLY NOT BECAUSE THEY CONFUSE **DO**G WITH **G**O**D**.

THERE'S ANOTHER SIMPLE REASON
WHY HESITANT READERS LEARN FASTER
WITH THE UPPERCASE ALPHABET:

26 < 52

BECAUSE 26 IS LESS THAN 52 !

THERE ARE HALF AS MANY LETTER FORMS TO MASTER
WHEN YOU READ ONLY UPPERCASE LETTERS.
THINK ABOUT IT.

MOST HIGHWAY SIGNS AND MANY SIGNS ON BUILDINGS
ARE WRITTEN IN CAPITAL LETTERS.

THAT MAY BE WHY EVEN THOSE WE HAVE THE AUDACITY
TO LABEL ILLITERATE OR LEARNING DISABLED
CAN READ   **STOP**
                  GO
                  BANK
                  BUS.

AND DON'T BE AFRAID THAT FOCUSING ON CAPITAL LETTERS
WILL HANDICAP YOUR LEARNING PARTNERS.
HALF OF THE UPPER AND LOWER CASE LETTERS
ARE ALIKE OR ALMOST ALIKE.
CHECK FOR YOURSELF.

THE FUNNY AND WONDERFUL THING IS
THAT THOSE WHO LEARN TO READ WITH CAPITAL LETTERS ONLY
VERY SOON FIND THEMSELVES
READING LOWERCASE LETTERS TOO AND WITH MUCH LESS EFFORT.

ONCE NEW READERS BEGIN TO GAIN SELF-CONFIDENCE
THEY WILL BEGIN TO DELVE INTO BOOKS
PRINTED THE TRADITIONAL WAY:
IN LOWERCASE LETTERS WITH INITIAL CAPS.

AND ONCE THEY'RE HOOKED ON BOOKS, WATCH OUT!

A B C D E F G H I J K L M N O P Q R S T U V W X Y Z

A
B
C
D
E
F
G
H
I
J
K
L
M
N
O
P
Q
R
S
T
U
V
W
X
Y
Z

ENVIRONMENTS ARE INVISIBLE
TO THOSE WHO ARE IN THEM.
--MARSHALL MCLUHAN

HERE'S SOME FOOD FOR THOUGHT:

Alongside a serious literacy problem
we have a longstanding publishing tradition:

Most alphabet books, basal readers
and easy-to-read stories
are printed in lowercase letters—
with initial caps, of course.

WHAT WOULD HAPPEN TO SALES
IF PUBLISHERS STARTED PRINTING
SOME, MANY, MOST OF THOSE BOOKS
IN CAPITAL LETTERS?

AFTER ALL, STATISTICS SAY THAT THERE ARE
MILLIONS AND MILLIONS OF NON-READERS OUT THERE.

FOR NOW, HOWEVER, LET'S EXPLORE THE COUNTER-CLAIM THAT
THERE ARE NO NON-READERS IN A PRINT-SATURATED SOCIETY.

EVERYONE RECOGNIZES **STOP**.
STOP IS A SIGHT WORD WRITTEN IN UPPERCASE LETTERS.
YOU CAN USE **STOP** AS A HOOK
ON WHICH TO HANG OTHER **OP** WORDS:

A B C D E F G H I J K L M N O P Q R S T U V W X Y Z

STOP
BOP
COP
HOP
MOP
POP
TOP

AS YOU BUILD THAT LIST WITH YOUR LEARNING PARTNERS
KEEP THE RHYMING LETTERS DIRECTLY UNDER EACH OTHER
AND THEY WILL BEGIN TO SEE HOW THE SYMBOL SYSTEM WORKS.
THEY WILL BEGIN TO EXPERIENCE WHAT DECODING IS ALL ABOUT.

A B C D E F G H I J K L M N O P Q R S T U V W X Y Z

A
B
C
D
E
F
G
H
I
J
K
L
M
N
O
P
Q
R
S
T
U
V
W
X
Y
Z

**NEVER
LET THE FEAR OF STRIKING OUT
GET IN YOUR WAY.
--*BABE RUTH***

74

TRY OTHER FAMILIAR SIGHT WORDS LIKE **BANK** AND **GO**.

A B C D E F G H I J K L M N O P Q R S T U V W X Y Z

> **BANK**
> HANK
> **RANK**
> **SANK**
> **TANK**

IF YOU AND YOUR LEARNING PARTNER ARE DARING
YOU CAN SIMULTANEOUSLY MAKE THREE **GO**-RELATED LISTS:
LISTS THAT CONTAIN SMALL WORDS, SOME FUN WORDS
AND A FEW WORDS THAT MAY INCREASE THEIR VOCABULARY.

A B C D E F G H I J K L M N O P Q R S T U V W X Y Z

GO	**BOW & ARROW**	**DOE**
HO!	**LOW**	**FOE**
NO	**ROW**	JOE
SO-SO	**SOW**	**TOE**
YO!	**TOW**	**WOE**
YOYO		

AS YOU ADD WORDS TO THE LISTS, MAKE SENTENCES WITH THEM.
DON'T BE AFRAID OF THE UNFAMILIAR OR STRANGE.
HAVE FUN WITH ALL THOSE RHYMING WORDS.
MAKE A LEARNING-NEW-WORDS GAME OUT OF IT.

AND SO WHAT IF THEY DON'T REMEMBER ALL OF THE NEW MEANINGS
OR CAN'T DECODE OR SPELL STRANGE WORDS ALL BY THEMSELVES.
WHY SHOULD THEY? THE HARD ONES MAY CLICK LATER—OR NOT.
THE FACT IS, YOU WILL HAVE TAKEN AWAY THE BOREDOM, THE FEAR
AND MADE THE DECODING PROCESS BOTH CHALLENGING AND FUN.

NOW, HOW MANY DIFFERENT LISTS CAN *YOU* MAKE WITH **OON**?
JUST FOR FUN, INCLUDE BOTH STRANGE AND POLYSYLLABIC WORDS
LIKE CONTRABASSOON, NEPTUNE, PANTALOON, RACCOON SASKATOON,
SPITTOON, TABLESPOON. AND DON'T FORGET STREWN.

LATER, WITH YOUR LEARNING PARTNER, HAVE FUN WITH **OOM**.
INSTEAD OF STARTING WITH BOOM AND BROOM
GO TO THE END OF THE ALPHABET: ZOOM, VROOM…AND TOMB?

A B C D E F G H I J K L M N O P Q R S T U V W X Y Z

A
B
C
D
E
F
G
H
I
J
K
L
M
N
O
P
Q
R
S
T
U
V
W
X
Y
Z

CHILDREN ARE NOT
THINGS TO BE MOLDED—
BUT PERSONS
TO BE UNFOLDED.
--ANONYMOUS

WHAT ABOUT SIGHT WORDS?

REMEMBER, ENGLISH IS FILLED WITH THOUSANDS OF WORDS
TAKEN FROM OTHER CULTURES.
UNLIKE SPANISH, IT IS NOT EASY TO SPELL SYLLABLE BY SYLLABLE.

COMPARE THESE FIVE WORDS:

BOUGH	COUGH	DOUGH	ROUGH	THROUGH
BOW?	COFF?	DOE?	RUFF?	THREW?

THEY MAY LOOK ALIKE, BUT THEY CERTAINLY DON'T SOUND ALIKE.

HOWEVER, IF YOU **BEGIN WITH THE KNOWN**
MANY HARD WORDS ARE EASY FOR NEW READERS
BECAUSE OF THE GUT CONNECTION, THE PERSONAL MEANING.

MUSTANG IS A GOOD EXAMPLE OF THE POWER OF SIGHT WORDS.
IF YOU SHOW A PICTURE OF A **HORSE**
WITH THE CAPTION **MUSTANG** UNDER IT
TO SOMEONE WHO KNOWS LITTLE ABOUT HORSES
AND WHO CAN'T READ
THE WORD MAY NOT BECOME A SIGHT WORD.

BUT, SHOW THAT SAME PERSON A **FORD MUSTANG**
WITH THE CAPTION **MUSTANG** UNDER IT
AND **MUSTANG** MAY BECOME A ONE-LOOK WORD
A HOOK ON WHICH TO HANG SEVERAL COLUMNS OF WORDS
WHICH YOU CAN BUILD AS YOU GO:

US
USS
UST

AND EVENTUALLY, **ANG**

HERE AGAIN IS ONE WAY TO **BUILD ON THE KNOWN**.

PRINT **US** AT THE TOP OF A NEW FILE CARD OR PAGE.
PLACE AN ALPHABET STRIP ABOVE IT
AND POINT TO **US** , SAYING:
"LET'S TAKE THE FIRST THREE LETTERS OF THE WORD **MUS**TANG."

A B C D E F G H I J K L M N O P Q R S T U V W X Y Z

A
B
C
D
E
F
G
H
I
J
K
L
M
N
O
P
Q
R
S
T
U
V
W
X
Y
Z

**PRAISE TO A CHILD
IS LIKE WATER
TO A THIRSTY PLANT.**
--ANONYMOUS

78

IF THEY KNOW IT'S PRONOUNCED **MUS**, FINE.

IF NOT, WITHOUT NAMING THE LETTERS, POINT TO THE **U** AND THE **S**.
SAY THE SOUNDS SLOWLY, IN SUCCESSION: **UH /S/**
HAVE THEM REPEAT: **U..S**

HAVE THEM REPEAT IT A BIT FASTER EACH TIME
AS YOU POINT TO THE **U** AND THEN THE **S** UNTIL **U..S** BECOMES **US**.
YES, **US!** YOU WILL SEE THE LIGHT BULB GO ON AT THAT POINT:

THAT IS WHAT **DECODING** IS ALL ABOUT:
TURNING LINES THAT ARE SYMBOLS INTO SOUND AND MEANING.

"LET'S MAKE A LIST OF **US** WORDS."
THEN POINT TO **B** ON THE ALPHABET STRIP:
"WHAT **US** WORD BEGINS WITH **/B/** ?" (VERY LIGHTLY; NOT BUH)

> TO AVOID OVERLOAD AT THIS POINT
> WITH THOSE VERY YOUNG LEARNING PARTNERS
> WHO MAY NOT KNOW ALL OF THE ALPHABET
> WORK WITH SOUNDS FIRST, RATHER THAN LETTER NAMES.
> ONCE CHILDREN RECOGNIZE THE SOUNDS
> THE LETTER NAMES WILL SOON FOLLOW.

WHEN THEY SAY **BUS**, ENTHUSIASTICALLY AGREE.
PRINT IT UNDER **US** **SO THAT THE DUPLICATED LETTERS ARE ALIGNED**
AND MOVE ON TO THE NEXT RELEVANT LETTER, **C**.

"WHAT **US** WORD BEGINS WITH **/K/** ?"
> (YES, THE **HARD C** SOUND, BUT SAY IT LIGHTLY.)
IF THEY SAY **CUSS**, INSTEAD OF SAYING THAT CUS IS NOT A WORD
> (REMEMBER, YOU ONLY HAVE ONE LIST SO FAR, THE **US** LIST)
ENTHUSIASTICALLY START ANOTHER COLUMN, CARD, PAGE
SAYING, "NOW YOU HAVE TWO LISTS GOING. FANTASTIC!"

DO THE SAME THING WITH **D**: **/D/** ? (LIGHTLY)
WHEN THEY SAY **"DUST?"** ENTHUSIASTICALLY START A THIRD LIST.

MOVING BACK AND FORTH FROM ONE LIST TO THE OTHER
CONTINUE GOING DOWN THE ALPHABET
WITH THE CONSONANT SOUNDS THAT BEGIN
US, USS, OR **UST** WORDS
AND YOU'LL BUILD THREE LISTS OF RHYMING WORDS
SIMULTANEOUSLY. WOW!

A B C D E F G H I J K L M N O P Q R S T U V W X Y Z

A
B
C
D
E
F
G
H
I
J
K
L
M
N
O
P
Q
R
S
T
U
V
W
X
Y
Z

AIN'T IT FUNNY
HOW YOU FEEL
WHEN YOU'RE FINDIN' OUT
IT'S REAL?
--*NEIL YOUNG*

NOW GO THROUGH THE CONSONANTS A SECOND TIME
AND ON A FOURTH CARD OR PAGE, LIST **ANG** WORDS
FROM THE SECOND SYLLABLE OF MUST**ANG**:

BANG
CLANG *
DANG
FANG ETC.

YOU WILL END UP WITH FOUR LISTS OF RHYMING WORDS
SIMILAR TO THESE, EACH LIST ON ITS OWN FILE CARD OR PAGE.

US	**CUSS**	**DUST**	**BANG**
BUS	**DISCUSS**	**JUST**	**CLANG** *
GUS	**FUSS**	**MUST**	**DANG**
MINIBUS	**RUSS**	**RUST**	**FANG**
PLUS *		**TRUST** *	**GANG**
PUS			**MUSTANG**
			RANG
			SANG
			TANG

AGAIN, DECODING IS ALL ABOUT
TURNING SIMPLE SYMBOLS...
      LINES (LONG, SHORT, VERTICAL, HORIZONTAL, DIAGONAL)
      CIRCLES AND CURVES (BIG, SMALL, FULL, PARTIAL)
      ANGLES (POINTING UP, DOWN, SIDEWAYS)
INTO SOUND AND INTO MEANING.

JUST AS ABOVE, MOVING FROM B TO C TO D
US BECAME BUS
      AND CUSS
      AND DUST
ENCOURAGE CREATIVITY WITH BOUNDLESS ENTHUSIASM.

RATHER THAN FORCE STRICT ADHERENCE TO A SAFE FORMULA
HAVE FUN WITH WORDS.
STRETCH YOUR LEARNING PARTNER'S MIND.
DON'T HESITATE TO ADD UNUSUAL OR POLYSYLLABIC WORDS:
THE WHOLE **SHEBANG**! **

---

* AS YOU BUILD MORE WORD FAMILY LISTS, BEGIN TO ADD **BLENDS,** WORDS THAT CONTAIN
  ARTICULATED CONSECUTIVE CONSONANTS, LIKE **CL**ANG, **PL**US, **TR**UST.

** YOU WILL SOON BE ABLE TO ADD **DIGRAPHS**, CONSECUTIVE CONSONANTS THAT PRODUCE
  A NEW AND DIFFERENT SOUND SEGMENT: **CH, GH, PH, SH, TH.**

A B C D E F G H I J K L M N O P Q R S T U V W X Y Z

A
B
C
D
E
F
G
H
I
J
K
L
M
N
O
P
Q
R
S
T
U
V
W
X
Y
Z

IF WE ARE TO ACHIEVE A RICHER CULTURE,
RICH IN CONTRASTING VALUES,
WE MUST RECOGNIZE THE WHOLE GAMUT OF HUMAN POTENTIAL
AND SO WEAVE A LESS ARBITRARY SOCIAL FABRIC,
ONE IN WHICH EACH DIVERSE HUMAN GIFT
WILL FIND A FITTING PLACE.
--*MARGARET MEAD*

82

<u>WHY</u> ENCOURAGE NEW READERS TO PASS IT ON?

ONCE YOUR LEARNING PARTNERS ARE COMFORTABLE WITH BOOKS
ONCE READING NO LONGER INTIMIDATES THEM, ASK THEM IF
NOW, OR DOWN THE ROAD A BIT, THEY WOULD BE WILLING
TO CONVERT THE LEARNING DYAD INTO A LEARNING TRIAD
AND ACCELERATE THEIR OWN LEARNING
BY **HELPING YOU TEACH A CHILD TO READ**.

THOSE WHO DECIDE TO GIVE IT A GO
WILL INDEED SEE THEIR OWN LEARNING ACCELERATE:

- MOVING FROM A DYAD TO A TRIAD, THEY WILL BECOME YOUR TUTORING PARTNER, AND YOU WILL MENTOR THEM IN THAT ROLE AS LONG AS THEY WISH.
- TOGETHER YOU WILL PLAN AND DEBRIEF EACH SESSION.
- THEY WILL BE ABLE TO WATCH A NEW READER'S SELF-CONFIDENCE INCREASE, AND THEY WILL KNOW THAT THEY HAVE MADE A DIFFERENCE.
- THEIR OWN SELF-CONFIDENCE AND COMMUNICATION SKILLS WILL GROW AS THEIR READING, WRITING, SPELLING, AND TUTORING SKILLS ARE ENHANCED.
- THEY WILL BEGIN TO EXPERIENCE THE EXHILARATION OF SEEING THAT WHEN WE HELP EACH OTHER LEARN, EVERYONE BENEFITS.

EVENTUALLY, EXPLAIN THE CONCEPT OF **GEOMETRIC PROGRESSION**:
IF YOU TEACH TWO LEARNING PARTNERS TO READ
AND, ONCE THEY ARE READY
IF THOSE TWO DECIDE TO TEACH TWO OTHERS IN THEIR LIFETIME
THEORETICALLY, THE NUMBERS COULD EXPAND
FROM 2 TO 4 TO 8 TO 16 TO 32 TO 64 TO 128 TO 256 TO 512 TO 1,024
AND ON AND ON AND ON.

HOWEVER, **REALITY SETS IN BECAUSE NO ONE MUST BE PRESSURED**.
IF SOMEONE WANTS TO GIVE IT A TRY, FINE. IF NOT, THAT'S FINE TOO.
SOME LEARNING PARTNERS MAY PREFER TO GET IN TOUCH WITH YOU LATER
TO PASS ON THE SKILLS THEY HAVE BECOME COMFORTABLE WITH.

IF NOT, END OF STORY. DO NOT INSIST. AT ALL.
THE MOST IMPORTANT VALUE IS TO RESPECT WHERE THEY ARE.

READING, BY ITS VERY NATURE
OPENS DOORS WITHIN AND BEYOND OURSELVES.
IT IS FOR EACH OF US TO DECIDE
WHICH DOORS WE WILL OPEN AND STEP THROUGH—AND WHEN.

A B C D E F G H I J K L M N O P Q R S T U V W X Y Z

A
B
C
D
E
F
G
H
I
J
K
L
M
N
O
P
Q
R
S
T
U
V
W
X
Y
Z

SECURITY IS MOSTLY SUPERSTITION.
IT DOES NOT EXIST IN NATURE
NOR DO CHILDREN OF MEN AS A WHOLE EXPERIENCE IT.
AVOIDING DANGER IS NOT SAFER IN THE LONG RUN
THAN OUTRIGHT EXPOSURE.
LIFE IS EITHER A DARING ADVENTURE
OR NOTHING.
--HELEN KELLER

HOW DO YOU MENTOR NEW TUTORS?

BEFORE EACH SESSION:

PLAN EACH SESSION TOGETHER.
ENCOURAGE NEW TUTORS TO NEVER HOLD BACK A QUESTION
BEFORE, DURING, OR AFTER A TUTORING SESSION.

MORE THAN LIKELY, THEY WILL WANT TO START SMALL.
AS THEY SHARE THE TUTORING WITH YOU
ENCOURAGE THEM TO TAKE ON ANY PART OF THE SESSION
WITH WHICH THEY FEEL COMFORTABLE.
THEY MAY OR MAY NOT TAKE ON A BIT MORE EACH TIME.

THE CHART AT THE END OF THIS BOOK MAY HELP YOU
BUT DON'T RUSH INTO THAT.
KEEP IT SIMPLE; AND KEEP THE TUTORING SESSIONS BRIEF.

AFTER EACH SESSION:

WHEN THE NEW LEARNING PARTNER LEAVES
YOU MAY WANT TO USE THE FOUR-LEVEL REFLECTION METHOD
TO GO OVER THE HIGHLIGHTS OF THE SESSION
WITH THE NEW TUTOR.

FACTS	WHAT STRUCK YOU? …OUR LEARNING PARTNER?
FEELINGS	WHERE WERE YOU COMFORTABLE? …OR NOT? WHAT WERE YOU SURPRISED BY? …PROUD OF?
LEARNINGS	WHAT DID WE LEARN AS WE TUTORED OUR LEARNING PARTNER? WHAT DID OUR PARTNER LEARN?
NEEDS/NEXT	WHAT WOULD YOU DO DIFFERENTLY NEXT TIME? WHAT WOULD YOU REVIEW AND CONTINUE TO DO?

AS YOU VARY YOUR QUESTIONS AND ANSWER THEIR QUESTIONS
KEEP IT SIMPLE
AND **LET THEM TALK AS MUCH AS THEY WANT TO**.
ABOVE ALL, LAVISH PRAISE, AND GIVE EACH OTHER A HIGH FIVE!

A B C D E F G H I J K L M N O P Q R S T U V W X Y Z

A
B
C
D
E
F
G
H
I
J
K
L
M
N
O
P
Q
R
S
T
U
V
W
X
Y
Z

YOU MISS 100%
OF THE SHOTS YOU NEVER TAKE.
--WAYNE GRETZKY

BETWEEN SESSIONS:

CONTINUE TUTORING THAT LEARNING PARTNER-TURNED-TUTOR.

NOW THERE IS AN EVEN STRONGER REASON
TO FOCUS
TO READ MORE
TO FORGE AHEAD.

WHY?
TO KEEP WELL AHEAD
OF *THEIR* NEW LEARNING PARTNER, OF COURSE. *

REMEMBER:

WE LEARN BEST WHAT WE TEACH.

YOU WILL SEE A SURGE OF GROWTH
SOMETIMES A SEA CHANGE
IN YOUR LEARNING PARTNERS' RELATIONSHIP
TO THE PRINTED WORD
TO LEARNING
TO THEMSELVES AND
TO THOSE WHO STRUGGLE TO LEARN.

LET THEM KNOW
THAT YOU SEE THE EFFORT
THE SUCCESS.

LAVISH PRAISE !

* TUTORS WHO USE FULLER'S SCIENCE FICTION STORYBOOKS MAY FIND, AFTER THEY HAVE COVERED 3 OR 4 OF THE 100+ PAGE BOOKS (WRITTEN AT A 3RD GRADE READING LEVEL AND ABOVE) , THAT EVEN SOME OF THEIR MUCH YOUNGER LEARNING PARTNERS ARE READY AND EAGER TO SHARE THEIR NEWFOUND KNOWLEDGE AND SKILL WITH ANOTHER CHILD AS PART OF A LEARNING TRIAD.

A B C D E F G H I J K L M N O P Q R S T U V W X Y Z

A
B
C
D
E
F
G
H
I
J
K
L
M
N
O
P
Q
R
S
T
U
V
W
X
Y
Z

MUST WEAKNESS BE CONCEALED
IN ORDER THAT RESPECT BE WON?...
MUST WE PRETEND TO FEARLESSNESS?
AND CERTAINTY?
SURELY EDUCATION SHOULD EQUIP US TO KNOW
WHAT TO FEAR
AND WHAT TO BE UNCERTAIN OF.
--*MARY CATHERINE RICHARDS*

<u>WHAT</u> DO YOU DO DURING THE NEW TUTOR'S SESSION?

TURN THE DYAD INTO A TRIAD.
ENCOURAGE YOUR NEW TUTORING PARTNER
TO INTRODUCE YOU AS THE ONE WHO IS HELPING THEM
TO FURTHER IMPROVE THEIR OWN READING SKILL
BY LEARNING HOW TO PASS IT ON.

ONE OR BOTH OF YOU WILL UNOBTRUSIVELY LIST THE WORDS
THAT THE NEW READER MISSES
ESPECIALLY THE EASIEST ONES.

THOSE WORDS COULD HAVE BEEN STUMBLING
    BLOCKS
HALTING THE
      FLOW OF THE
   STORY.

BUT YOUR TUTORING PARTNER (OR YOU, IF THEY HESITATED)
GAVE THEM THE WORDS THAT ALLOWED THEM TO KEEP GOING.

WHEN THE NEW READER IS READY TO STOP
YOUR TUTORING PARTNER MAY DECIDE TO DEFER TO YOU
TO TEACH THE WORDS THAT RHYME
WITH SOME OF THE WORDS MISSED.
OR YOU MAY ALTERNATE.

AS BEFORE, YOU WILL ACCELERATE LEARNING
IF YOU LEAVE OUT THE MORE DIFFICULT WORDS
FOR WHICH THE NEW READER IS NOT YET READY
AND START WITH THE EASIEST WORDS.

EITHER OF YOU MAY EXPLAIN
HOW EACH SET OF RHYMING WORDS
WILL HAVE ITS OWN FILE CARD
      OR ITS OWN PAGE IN A SMALL NOTEBOOK
TO USE AND ADD TO AT EACH SESSION.
THOSE NEW WORDS WILL BECOME BASIC BUILDING BLOCKS
CRAFTED FROM ORDINARY OLD STUMBLING BLOCKS.

AS THE THREE OF YOU WORK TOGETHER
YOU WILL ALL LEARN TOGETHER.

A B C D E F G H I J K L M N O P Q R S T U V W X Y Z

A
B
C
D
E
F
G
H
I
J
K
L
M
N
O
P
Q
R
S
T
U
V
W
X
Y
Z

I REMEMBER
10% OF WHAT I READ
20% OF WHAT I HEAR
30% OF WHAT I SEE
50% OF WHAT I SEE AND HEAR
70% OF WHAT I DISCUSS WITH OTHERS
80% OF WHAT I EXPERIENCE BY DOING
95% OF WHAT I TEACH TO OTHERS.
--SUSAN KOVALIK

ONCE THEY ARE COMFORTABLE LEADING MUCH OF THE SESSION
YOU CAN LITERALLY BEGIN TO PULL BACK
SITTING SLIGHTLY BEHIND PERHAPS, OUT OF THE LIMELIGHT
SPEAKING SOFTLY AND AS LITTLE AS NECESSARY.

BE A QUIET, HELPFUL PRESENCE
UNTIL THE DAY THE NEW TUTOR TELLS YOU:
"NEXT TIME WE MEET WITH OUR LEARNING PARTNER
I WANT TO TRY IT ON MY OWN."

THEN, BE THERE STILL, IN THE SAME ROOM
BUT NO LONGER PART OF A TRIAD.
BRING SOME WORK TO DO. BE AN UNOBTRUSIVE OBSERVER.
AND BE SURE TO TAKE NOTES SO THAT YOU CAN PROVIDE
>   POSITIVE FEEDBACK
>   HELPFUL SUGGESTIONS
WHEN YOU DEBRIEF THAT SESSION AND PREPARE FOR THE NEXT ONE.

ONCE YOUR LEARNING PARTNERS TRY THEIR WINGS
THEY WILL HAVE BECOME A NEW SIGN OF HOPE AND POSSIBILITY
TO CHILDREN, YOUTH, AND ADULTS
WHO HAVE HAD DIFFICULTY LEARNING TO READ.

BOTH OF YOU WILL HAVE BEGUN TO BUILD
A GEOMETRIC PROGRESSION OF LEARNING IN YOUR OWN BACKYARD.

BY MOTIVATING YOUR LEARNING PARTNERS
TO BELIEVE IN THEMSELVES ENOUGH
TO WANT TO PASS ON WHAT THEY HAVE LEARNED
YOU WILL DEMONSTRATE THAT
>   **THE COMMUNITY OF NEED CAN INDEED**
>   **BECOME THE COMMUNITY OF SERVICE.**

AND BOTH OF YOU WILL BE PART OF
>   AN INFORMAL NETWORK OF INDIVIDUALS
>   A GROWING COALITION OF LEARNING PARTNERS *
>   WITH A COMMITMENT
>   TO LEARN FROM EACH OTHER AND
>   TO PASS IT ON:

EACH OF YOU TEACH TWO!

* TO HELP BUILD THAT COALITION, JOIN THE DIALOGUE AT www.teachtwo.net

A B C D E F G H I J K L M N O P Q R S T U V W X Y Z

A
B
C
D
E
F
G
H
I
J
K
L
M
N
O
P
Q
R
S
T
U
V
W
X
Y
Z

IF ONE MAN DIES,
IT IS A TRAGEDY;
IF A THOUSAND MEN DIE,
IT IS A STATISTIC.
--*PHILIPPE BERTHELOT*

<u>WHAT</u> COULD *EACH OF YOU TEACH TWO!* DO ?

EACH OF YOU TEACH TWO!
COULD BEGIN TO WIPE OUT LOW LITERACY IN A CLASSROOM
IF EVERY HESITANT READER
WERE PAIRED WITH A TEACHER'S AIDE

OR AN OLDER STUDENT
A COLLEGE STUDENT
A PARENT
AN ELDER
SOMEONE WHO BELIEVES IN PASSING IT ON.

EACH OF YOU TEACH TWO!
COULD BEGIN TO WIPE OUT LOW LITERACY IN TWO CLASSROOMS
BY PAIRING HESITANT YOUNGER READERS
WITH OLDER STUDENTS
FROM REMEDIAL OR SPECIAL EDUCATION PROGRAMS

STUDENTS WHO WERE TRAINED AND ENCOURAGED TO PASS IT ON
WITH A TUTOR-TURNED-MENTOR
—WHO MIGHT EVEN BE A MAINSTREAMED PEER—AT THEIR SIDE.

EACH OF YOU TEACH TWO!
COULD BEGIN TO WIPE OUT LOW LITERACY IN A PRISON
OR A JUVENILE INSTITUTION
IF WILLING HESITANT READERS
WERE PAIRED WITH PEER TUTORS FROM INSIDE
OR VOLUNTEER TUTORS FROM OUTSIDE THE WALLS…

AND IF WILLING NEW READERS
WERE EVENTUALLY TAUGHT HOW TO TEACH TWO OTHERS TO READ
AND ENCOURAGED TO DO SO
WITH THEIR TUTOR-TURNED-MENTOR AT THEIR SIDE.

WHAT DO YOU THINK? MIGHT YOU ENCOURAGE SOMEONE TO PASS IT ON?
AS HENRY FORD SAID,
"IF YOU THINK YOU CAN OR YOU CAN'T,
YOU'RE ALWAYS RIGHT."

ABCDEFGHIJKLMNOPQRSTUVWXYZ

A
B
C
D
E
F
G
H
I
J
K
L
M
N
O
P
Q
R
S
T
U
V
W
X
Y
Z

BOTH LEARNER AND TEACHER UNDERGO CHANGE.
THE CHANGE IS IRREVERSIBLE AND PROFOUND.
THE WORLD WILL NEVER BE THE SAME AGAIN—
NOT FOR THE ONE,
NOT FOR THE OTHER.
THE SILENCE IS BROKEN.
--JONATHAN KOZOL

LISTENING

THE SINGLE MOST ESSENTIAL SKILL FOR LITERACY ACCELERATION IS THE CAPACITY TO GENUINELY LISTEN—WITH YOUR EYES AND WITH YOUR HEART—TO YOURSELF AND TO YOUR LEARNING PARTNERS. YOU WILL BECOME REAL LEARNING PARTNERS ONCE YOU ARE OPEN TO LEARNING AS MUCH FROM THEM AS THEY DO FROM YOU.

GENUINE LISTENING CREATES SAFE SPACE AND TAKES AWAY THE ANXIETY THAT INHIBITS LEARNING. WHEN YOU FEEL SAFE, YOU ARE OPEN TO NEW THOUGHTS AND NEW POSSIBILITIES. DIFFICULTIES BECOME, NOT A THREAT TO AVOID AND DENY, BUT A CHALLENGE TO FACE—OR TO CONSCIOUSLY DECIDE NOT TO FACE JUST YET. WHEN YOU FEEL SAFE YOU DON'T HAVE TO APOLOGIZE OR PRETEND. IN FACT, PAST PERFORMANCE MAKES LITTLE DIFFERENCE. A NEW WORLD OF LEARNING OPENS UP.

GENUINE LISTENING ALSO ALLOWS YOU TO DISCOVER YOUR GREATEST RESOURCE: YOUR PARTNERS' LIFE EXPERIENCES AND REAL INTERESTS AND YOUR OWN. WHEN YOUR LEARNING PARTNERS ARE ALLOWED TO FOLLOW THEIR DEEPEST INTERESTS, THEY CAN FOCUS MORE EASILY AND LEARNING BECOMES ORGANIC. IF YOU LET THEIR ENTHUSIASM AND THE LIGHT IN THEIR EYES GUIDE YOU, MOTIVATION WILL BECOME SELF-DIRECTED AND SELF-REINFORCING. JUST LISTEN FOR CLUES ABOUT THEIR NEW OR HIDDEN INTERESTS TO POINT YOU TO BOOKS, MAGAZINES, NEWSPAPERS, AND OTHER MATERIALS CONTAINING WORDS AND PHRASES THAT THEY DON'T KNOW THEY KNOW.

HAVE THE COURAGE TO IMMEDIATELY DROP ANYTHING THAT IS OF NO INTEREST OR SMACKS OF BUSYWORK. THE MOTIVATION TO LEARN WILL THEN ACCELERATE.

PARADOXICALLY, HOW WELL YOU LISTEN TO YOUR DEEPEST SELF WILL BE THE MEASURE OF HOW WELL YOU HEAR WHAT YOUR LEARNING PARTNERS SHARE WITH YOU. ALLOW YOURSELF TO TRUST YOUR OWN INSTINCTS, INSIGHTS, AND INTERESTS.

AS YOU BECOME MORE CONSCIOUS OF THE LEARNINGS FROM YOUR OWN LIFE EXPERIENCE, THE TIME YOU SPEND TOGETHER WILL BE GREATLY ENRICHED. YOU WILL DISCOVER THE SYNERGY OF TWO PEOPLE ENGAGED IN A COMMON TASK. YOU WILL EXPERIENCE A LEVEL OF HEARTFELT RESPONSIVENESS AND PRODUCTIVE CREATIVITY THAT MAY BE NEW TO BOTH OF YOU.

A B C D E F G H I J K L M N O P Q R S T U V W X Y Z

A
B
C
D
E
F
G
H
I
J
K
L
M
N
O
P
Q
R
S
T
U
V
W
X
Y
Z

SERVICE IS THE RENT YOU PAY
FOR ROOM ON THIS EARTH.
IF PEOPLE NEED YOUR HELP,
YOU HELP.
--SHIRLEY CHISHOLM

COMMUNITY-BASED LITERACY

COMMUNITY-BASED LITERACY IS A TIMELY, LOW-COST, RESULTS-ORIENTED PARTNERSHIP WHOSE TIME HAS COME. YOU CAN JOIN THE RANKS OF THOSE WHO DARE TO MAKE IT SO BY TAKING WHAT YOU KNOW AND SHARING IT WITH CHILDREN, YOUTH, OR EVEN ADULTS WHO WERE MISLED INTO BELIEVING THAT THEY ARE NOT INTELLIGENT, NOT CAPABLE OF LEARNING TO READ.

VOLUNTEER AT A LIBRARY, SCHOOL, SHELTER, PRISON. VOLUNTEER AT A NEIGHBORHOOD OR COMMUNITY CENTER, AT AN AFTER-SCHOOL PROGRAM, OR AT A PROGRAM AFFILIATED WITH A SYNAGOGUE, MOSQUE, OR CHURCH.

START SMALL AND TRUST YOURSELF. THEN YOU WILL BE ABLE TO TRUST YOUR LEARNING PARTNERS. YOU HAVE NO IDEA HOW MUCH YOUR LIFE WILL BE ENRICHED, AS WILL THEIRS.

TUTOR JUST ONE CHILD OR ADULT, AND YOU WILL HAVE **TOUCHED THE FUTURE**! AND IF THAT ONE LEARNING PARTNER DECIDES SOMEDAY TO PASS ON TO ONE OR TWO OTHERS WHAT YOU HAVE TAUGHT THEM, YOU MAY HAVE BEGUN A GEOMETRIC PROGRESSION OF LEARNING.

WORKING TOGETHER WE CAN BEGIN TO WIPE OUT LOW LITERACY.

JOIN THE GRASSROOTS MOVEMENT TO

TURN THE COMMUNITY OF NEED INTO THE COMMUNITY OF SERVICE.

EACH OF YOU TEACH TWO!

A B C D E F G H I J K L M N O P Q R S T U V W X Y Z

A
B
C
D
E
F
G
H
I
J
K
L
M
N
O
P
Q
R
S
T
U
V
W
X
Y
Z

**FIND THE GOOD
AND PRAISE IT.**
--ALEX HALEY

ACKNOWLEDGEMENTS

A LOVING TRIBUTE TO MY MOTHER, **ALFREDA TESSIER NOEL**. SHE READ TO US CONSTANTLY DURING MANY CHILDHOOD ILLNESSES, ESPECIALLY THE WONDERFUL ANIMAL TALES OF **THORNTON W. BURGESS** FROM CAPE COD IN OUR HOME STATE. THOSE STORIES REVEALED TO CLAUDIA, FRED, AND ME A WORLD OF PLUCK AND COLOR-BLIND PARTNERSHIP AND INSTILLED IN US A LIFELONG LOVE OF READING.

WARM THANKS TO MY FRIEND, CHILDHOOD NEIGHBOR, AND CERTIFIED READING TEACHER, **ANDI MANIATIS,** FOR SHARING WITH ME HER EXPERTISE AND HER PASSION FOR TEACHING READING.

LITERACY VOLUNTEERS OF AMERICA FOUNDER, RUTH COLVIN, ENCOURAGED TUTORS TO USE THE **LANGUAGE EXPERIENCE APPROACH (LEA)**: "I TELL YOU MY STORY, YOU WRITE IT DOWN, AND WOW! I CAN READ IT!" THAT SIMPLE TOOL OPENED UP A WHOLE NEW WORLD OF POSSIBILITY TO THE WOMEN I TUTORED WHEN I SAT ON THE LVA/ CAMDEN COUNTY (NJ) BOARD AND TO THE HUNDREDS OF UNDERGRADUATES I TRAINED AT RUTGERS UNIVERSITY'S CAMDEN CAMPUS.

I SAW THE MOST AMAZING FRUITS OF LANGUAGE EXPERIENCE WHEN I MET **BILL KNAKE** AT **DEE DICKINSON'S** NEW HORIZONS FOR LEARNING CONFERENCE IN TACOMA, WA. ALREADY IN HIS 30S, BILL HAD BEEN READING FOR LESS THAN A YEAR. VERY EARLY ON, BILL TOLD HIS TUTOR, **LINDA CAMPBELL**, THAT HE WANTED TO WRITE A BOOK ABOUT HIS 12 YEARS IN A STATE INSTITUTION FOR THE MENTALLY RETARDED. BILL TOLD LINDA HIS STORY, SHE WROTE DOWN HIS WORDS, AND SOON HE ASKED HER FOR A TYPEWRITER. BILL TYPED THE 50+ PAGES HIMSELF AND SOLD *THE INSIDE WORLD* AT THE CONFERENCE FOR $2. I HAVE SHARED HIS BOOK WITH COUNTLESS CLASSES.

LINDA AND BILL INTRODUCED ME TO **DR. RENÉE FULLER'S** WORK, AND EVERYTHING OPENED UP. EIGHT OF FULLER'S TEN WHIMSICAL DR. SEUSS-LIKE BOOKS ARE PRINTED IN CAPITAL LETTERS; AND **WITH HER SYSTEM OF UPPERCASE LETTERS THERE ARE NO REVERSALS.**

WITH FULLER'S BOOKS, FOR 15 TO 20 MINUTES AT BEDTIME ONCE A WEEK, I TAUGHT MY ADOPTED TWIN SONS HOW TO READ AFTER OVER THREE YEARS OF HELPLESSNESS ON MY PART, SUCCESSFUL TEACHER THOUGH I WAS IN OTHER AREAS. EACH IN THEIR RESPECTIVE CLASSROOMS, ONE BOY WAS NAMED **MOST IMPROVED WRITER** FOUR MONTHS AFTER WE STARTED, AND THREE MONTHS LATER, THE OTHER WAS NAMED **MOST IMPROVED READER**. AFTER COVERING SIX OF THE TEN 100-PAGE BOOKS IN NINE MONTHS, WITH FEWER THAN 20 TOTAL HOURS OF TUTORING, STANDARDIZED CLASSROOM ASSESSMENTS REVEALED THAT THEY HAD EACH GAINED OVER TWO GRADE LEVELS.

OVER THE SUMMER THREE MONTHS LATER, AND WITH JUST 20 MINUTES' INITIAL COACHING IN BOOK ONE, THE TWINS PASSED IT ON TO SIX-YEAR-OLD **LAURA ESPOSITO** WHOSE PARENTS ARE BLIND. **DAVID** MET WITH HER FIVE TIMES FOR 20 MINUTES, THEN **DANIEL**. TWO YEARS LATER, WITH FULLER'S BOOKS AND WITH NO PROMPTING OR HELP, LAURA TAUGHT A SIX-YEAR-OLD FRIEND TO READ.

COUNTLESS HARD-WORKING TEACHERS AND CONCERNED PARENTS HAVE INSPIRED ME TO WRITE THIS BOOK—ESPECIALLY THOSE WHO, LIKE ME, DIDN'T, OR DON'T YET, KNOW SIMPLE, PROVEN WAYS TO TEACH A CHILD TO READ FROM SCRATCH. I WAS ONE OF YOU. I KNOW.

JOAN LAZAR WAS DIRECTOR OF THE NEWARK (NJ) LITERACY CAMPAIGN WHEN, AT A RUTGERS READING CONFERENCE, SHE CLAIMED THAT **THERE ARE NO NON-READERS IN A PRINT-SATURATED SOCIETY; THERE ARE, HOWEVER, MILLIONS WHO DON'T KNOW THAT THEY KNOW.** AT THE NEWARK PUBLIC LIBRARY A FEW MONTHS LATER, AS I WATCHED HER WORK ONE-ON-ONE WITH ADULTS, I REALIZED THAT, ALTHOUGH OUR APPROACH AND METHODS DIFFER, HER WORDS WERE NO IDLE CLAIM.

DR. MARY ARNOLD FRAZIER, DR. WILMA FARMER, AND LINNELL WRIGHT WELCOMED ME INTO THE **CAMDEN SCHOOL DISTRICT** TO TRAIN PARENTS AND PROFESSIONALS. WHEN FEDERAL FUNDING FOR THE STUDENT LITERACY CORPS STOPPED, THEY PROVIDED EMERGENCY FINANCIAL SUPPORT. THEN, THROUGH AMERICA READS, 3RD AND 8TH GRADERS IN REMEDIAL AND SPECIAL EDUCATION PROGRAMS LEARNED TO TUTOR THEIR PEERS AND YOUNGER MAINSTREAMED HESITANT READERS.

AT RUTGERS, **KATHRYN BLACKSHEAR AND VERNA CARROWAY** TOOK MY URBAN LITERACY PRACTICUM AND, AS THEIR 50-HOUR TUTORING REQUIREMENT, STARTED AN AFTER-SCHOOL HOMEWORK PROGRAM AT THE CHELTON TERRACE HOUSING DEVELOPMENT IN SOUTH CAMDEN, WHERE KATHRYN WAS PRESIDENT OF THE TENANT ASSOCIATION. A FEW YEARS LATER, GRANTS FROM THE **CAMPBELL SOUP FOUNDATION** ALLOWED ME TO HIRE KATHRYN AS PROGRAM MANAGER AND TWO OTHER RESIDENTS, **DEBBIE KEYES AND REBECCA WARE**, AS SUPERVISORS FOR TWO SUMMER-LONG LITERACY PROGRAMS WHERE OLDER YOUTH TUTORED CHILDREN WITH FULLER'S BOOKS. DURING THE SECOND SUMMER, I BEGAN TO TEACH THE CHILDREN, YOUTH, AND SOME PARENTS WHAT I WAS TEACHING MY COLLEGE LITERACY STUDENTS.

OVER THE YEARS I WORKED IN SEVERAL COUNTRIES WITH THE **INSTITUTE OF CULTURAL AFFAIRS** (ICA). THAT INTERNATIONAL COMMUNITY DEVELOPMENT ORGANIZATION ENRICHED MY REAL WORLD LEARNING AND TEACH-ING FAR BEYOND MY FORMAL EDUCATION. THE **FOUR-LEVEL REFLECTION** IS ONE OF ICA'S EXTENSIVE ARRAY OF SIMPLE GRASSROOTS LEADERSHIP METHODS.

I WAS ON RECEPTIONIST DUTY AT ICA HEADQUARTERS IN CHICAGO IN 1977 WHEN AN ELDERLY STRANGER WITH A KNAPSACK INTRODUCED HIMSELF AS **MYLES HORTON**. I KNEW NOTHING OF MYLES AND ZILPHIA HORTON'S HIGHLANDER FOLK SCHOOL NOR OF THE ROLE THAT MYLES HAD PLAYED IN THE LIFE OF **SEPTIMA CLARK AND THE CITIZENSHIP SCHOOLS** IN THE DEEP SOUTH AND IN THE LIVES OF THE LEADERS OF THE CIVIL RIGHTS MOVEMENT. HORTON AND CLARK HAVE HAD A DEEP IMPACT ON MY VISION OF **THE UNTAPPED POWER AND POSSIBILITY OF GRASSROOTS LITERACY AND ACTION**, AS HAVE THE LIFE WORK AND WRITINGS OF **MARVA COLLINS, JAMES P. COMER, PAULO FREIRE, HERB KOHL, AND JONATHAN KOZOL**.

SYLVIA ASHTON-WARNER'S MID-CENTURY CLASSIC, *TEACHER,* INTRODUCED ME TO SIMPLE, **ORGANIC METHODS** WHICH, LIKE FULLER'S WORK, MOVE BEYOND THE LIMITATIONS OF TRADITIONAL BASAL READERS. SEARCHERS AND SKEPTICS ALIKE REVEL IN ASHTON-WARNER'S LOVING, LUCID TALE OF ACCELERATED READING AND WRITING AMONG MAORI PRE-SCHOOLERS.

I HAVE BEEN DEEPLY INSPIRED BY **JOHN MAHER AND MIMI SILBERT'S DELANCEY STREET FOUNDATION**. AVERAGE NEWCOMERS ARE **FUNCTIONALLY ILLITERATE**. WITH NO OUTSIDE FUNDING AND NO PAID STAFF, THOUSANDS OF CONVICTS, ADDICTS, AND HOMELESS MEN AND WOMEN OBTAIN A GED, LEARN THREE MARKETABLE SKILLS, THEN **TEACH EACH OTHER**. THE ORGANIZATION IS **RUN BY RESIDENTS** WHO, BY POOLING THEIR RESOURCES, HAVE BUILT A MULTI-FACETED, MULTI-MILLION DOLLAR, AWARD-WINNING CORPORATION, GRADUATING OVER 14,000 PRODUCTIVE, TAX-PAYING CITIZENS WHO LIVE AND WORK IN FIVE AMERICAN CITIES.

SPECIAL THANKS TO MY NEIGHBORS DOWN THE ROAD, **DR. ALTON WILLIAMS AND HIS WIFE, BONNIE**, WHO INTRODUCED ME TO **VISION THERAPY** AND INVITED ME TO JOIN THEM AT THEIR OPTOMETRY OFFICE ON SATURDAY MORNINGS WITH MY LITERACY KIT BAG. VOLUNTEERS, WORKING ONE-ON-ONE, PUT ENTHUSIASTIC CHILDREN AND YOUTH THROUGH A SERIES OF GAME-LIKE EXERCISES TO IMPROVE THEIR HAND-EYE COORDINATION AND THEIR ABILITY TO FOCUS THEIR EYES AND THEIR ATTENTION. THE RESULTS ARE LITERALLY IN THEIR EYES, IN THEIR BEHAVIOR, AND ON THEIR REPORT CARDS.

LASTLY, THE FOCUS OF THIS BOOK ON THE IRREPLACEABLE ROLE OF SAFE SPACE AND PERSONAL CHOICE IN BRAIN DEVELOPMENT AND MEANINGFUL LEARNING OWES MUCH AND IS A TRIBUTE TO **PAUL MacLEAN'S TRIUNE BRAIN THEORY AND MALCOLM KNOWLES'S WORK ON ANDRAGOGY**. EVERY TRUE EDUCATOR KNOWS THAT SELF-MOTIVATED, SELF-DIRECTED LEARNING IS AS TRANSFORMATIVE FOR CHILDREN AS IT IS FOR ADULTS. THANKS DAN, DAVE, AND LAURA FOR LEADING THE WAY AND FOR SHOWING US OLD-TIMERS WHAT IS POSSIBLE.

A B C D E F G H I J K L M N O P Q R S T U V W X Y Z

A
B
C
D
E
F
G
H
I
J
K
L
M
N
O
P
Q
R
S
T
U
V
W
X
Y
Z

THE LECTURE
IS A LATE MEDIEVAL INVENTION
INSTITUTED BECAUSE BOOKS WERE SCARCE.
--ANN E. BERTHOFF

A READING LIST AND SOME WEBSITES

WALTER ANDERSON
READ WITH ME: THE POWER OF READING—AND HOW IT TRANSFORMS OUR LIVES

THOMAS ARMSTRONG
THE MYTH OF THE A.D.D. CHILD: 50 WAYS TO IMPROVE YOUR CHILD'S BEHAVIOR & ATTENTION SPAN WITHOUT DRUGS, LABELS OR COERCION

SYLVIA ASHTON-WARNER
TEACHER

COLLEEN DUNN BATES AND SUSAN LATEMPA
STORYBOOK TRAVELS

ERMA BOMBECK
THE BEST OF BOMBECK

CYNTHIA BROWN
READY FROM WITHIN: SEPTIMA CLARK AND THE CIVIL RIGHTS MOVEMENT

MARC BROWN
*ARTHUR'S READING RACE [WHICH D.W. WINS W/**CAPS**!]*

THORNTON W. BURGESS
MOTHER WEST WIND STORIES TO READ ALOUD

TONY BUZAN
USE BOTH SIDES OF YOUR BRAIN (MINDMAPPING)

BEN CARSON, MD WITH CECIL MURPHEY
GIFTED HANDS: THE BEN CARSON STORY

JOHN CIARDI
YOU READ TO ME, I'LL READ TO YOU

SANDRA CISNEROS
THE HOUSE ON MANGO STREET

MARVA COLLINS AND CIVIA TAMARKIN
MARVA COLLINS' WAY

JAMES P. COMER
MAGGIE'S AMERICAN DREAM

BILL COSBY
CHILDHOOD; FATHERHOOD; KIDS SAY THE DARNDEST THINGS; LITTLE BILL

BERNICE E. CULLINAN
READ TO ME: RAISING KIDS WHO LOVE TO READ

RONALD D. DAVIS, ET AL.
THE GIFT OF LEARNING: PROVEN NEW METHODS FOR CORRECTING ADD, MATH, AND HANDWRITING PROBLEMS

DEE DICKINSON
NEW HORIZONS FOR LEARNING www.newhorizons.org

BOBBI DEPORTER WITH MIKE HERNACKI www.learningforum.com
QUANTUM LEARNING: UNLEASHING THE GENIUS IN YOU

STEPHEN DUNNING, EDWARD LEUDERS, HUGH SMITH
REFLECTIONS ON A GIFT OF WATERMELON PICKLE…AND OTHER MODERN VERSE

RIANE EISLER AND DAVID LOYE
THE PARTNERSHIP WAY: NEW TOOLS FOR LIVING AND LEARNING

PETER ELBOW
WRITING WITHOUT TEACHERS

DANIEL FADER, ET AL.
THE NEW HOOKED ON BOOKS

MEM FOX
READING MAGIC: WHY READING ALOUD TO OUR CHILDREN WILL CHANGE THEIR LIVES FOREVER

PAULO FREIRE
PEDAGOGY OF THE OPPRESSED

RENÉE FULLER   www.ballstickbird.com
IN SEARCH OF THE IQ CORRELATION

JUNE GOULD
THE WRITER IN ALL OF US: IMPROVING YOUR WRITING THROUGH CHILDHOOD MEMORIES

CHARLES HAMPDEN-TURNER
SANE ASYLUM (THE DELANCEY STREET FOUNDATION)

THOM HARTMANN
ATTENTION DEFICIT DISORDER: A DIFFERENT PERCEPTION

MYLES HORTON AND PAULO FREIRE
WE MAKE THE ROAD BY WALKING: CONVERSATIONS ON EDUCATION AND SOCIAL CHANGE

MYLES HORTON WITH JUDITH AND HERBERT KOHL
THE LONG HAUL: THE AUTOBIOGRAPHY OF MYLES HORTON

PETER KLINE
THE EVERYDAY GENIUS: RESTORING CHILDREN'S NATURAL JOY OF LEARNING, AND YOURS TOO

KENNETH KOCH
WISHES, LIES, AND DREAMS: TEACHING CHILDREN TO WRITE POETRY

HERB KOHL
READING: HOW TO

JONATHAN KOZOL
PRISONERS OF SILENCE: BREAKING THE BONDS OF ADULT LITERACY IN THE US

THOMAS KUHN
THE STRUCTURE OF SCIENTIFIC REVOLUTIONS

DAVID LAZEAR
THE MULTIPLE INTELLIGENCES WAY

RICHARD LEDERER
THE MIRACLE OF LANGUAGE
CRAZY ENGLISH: THE ULTIMATE JOY RIDE THROUGH OUR LANGUAGE
KEN MACRORIE
UPTAUGHT
MALCOLM X
THE AUTOBIOGRAPHY OF MALCOLM X AS TOLD TO ALEX HALEY
DAVID MELTON
A BOY CALLED HOPELESS, BY MJ
DONNA JO NAPOLI
THE PRINCE OF THE POND, OTHERWISE KNOWN AS DE FAWG PIN
JOSEPH CHILTON PEARCE
MAGICAL CHILD
MARY TAYLOR PREVITE
HUNGRY GHOSTS: ONE WOMAN'S MISSION TO CHANGE THEIR WORLD
PROLITERACY WORLDWIDE/PROLITERACY AMERICA www.proliteracy.org
FOR LOCAL PROGRAMS: www.proliteracy.org/locator
BARBARA REED
FOOD, TEENS & BEHAVIOR
GABRIELE RICO
WRITING THE NATURAL WAY (MINDMAPPING)
ANTOINE DE SAINT-EXUPÉRY
THE LITTLE PRINCE
ALVIN SCHWARTZ
TOMFOOLERY: TRICKERY AND FOOLERY WITH WORDS COLLECTED FROM AMERICAN FOLKLORE
ILENE SEGALOVE AND PAUL BOB VELICK
LIST YOUR SELF: LISTMAKING AS THE WAY TO SELF-DISCOVERY
DR. SEUSS
CHOOSE YOUR FAVORITES…
DOROTHY STRICKLAND
LISTEN CHILDREN: AN ANTHOLOGY OF BLACK LITERATURE
JIM TRELEASE
HEY! LISTEN TO THIS: STORIES TO READ ALOUD; THE READ-ALOUD HANDBOOK
RAYMUNDO VERAS
CHILDREN OF DREAMS, CHILDREN OF HOPE
VERIZON LITERACY UNIVERSITY www.vluonline.org
JUDITH VIORST
ALEXANDER AND THE TERRIBLE, HORRIBLE, NO GOOD, VERY BAD DAY; IF I WERE IN CHARGE OF THE WORLD
WEBSTER'S *COMPACT RHYMING DICTIONARY: A MERRIAM-WEBSTER DICTIONARY*

A Note on Undetected Vision Problems

RESEARCH SHOWS THAT, **WITH OR WITHOUT GLASSES**, APPROXIMATELY **1 OUT OF 4 CHILDREN AND 7 OUT OF 10 JUVENILE DELINQUENTS** HAVE VISION PROBLEMS WHICH INTERFERE WITH THE BRAIN'S ABILITY TO PROCESS WHAT IS SEEN. FEW SPECIALISTS PRACTICE A DEVELOPMENTAL APPROACH TO VISION CARE THROUGH **VISION THERAPY EXERCISES** THAT IMPROVE THE ABILITY TO FOCUS ATTENTION AND STIMULATE EYE-BRAIN ACTIVITY AND COORDINATION. FOR A STATEWIDE LIST OF OPTOMETRISTS CERTIFIED TO DO VISION THERAPY, ENTER JUST THE NAME OF YOUR STATE AT covd.org/membersearch.php, WEBSITE OF THE COLLEGE OF OPTOMETRISTS IN VISION DEVELOPMENT.

FOR FURTHER INFORMATION, SEE THE WEBSITE OF P.A.V.E., PARENTS ACTIVE FOR VISION EDUCATION: www.pavevision.org,

EACH OF YOU TEACH TWO!

JOIN THE LITERACY DIALOGUE ON OUR WEBSITE

www.teachtwo.net

IF I AM NOT FOR MYSELF, WHO IS FOR ME?
IF I AM ONLY FOR MYSELF, WHAT AM I?
IF NOT NOW, WHEN?
--Rabbi Hiillel

LUCILLE T. CHAGNON, M.ED.

COMMUNITY-BASED LITERACY HAS BEEN LUCILLE CHAGNON'S PASSION EVER SINCE SHE TAUGHT HER TEN-YEAR-OLD ADOPTED TWIN SONS TO READ, AND THREE MONTHS LATER THEY TAUGHT A SIX-YEAR-OLD WHO, WHEN SHE WAS EIGHT, TAUGHT ANOTHER SIX-YEAR-OLD TO READ.

A ONE-TIME INNER-CITY PRINCIPAL AND LONGTIME TEACHER IN FIVE STATES, LUCILLE TAUGHT A THREE-CREDIT URBAN LITERACY PRACTICUM AT RUTGERS UNIVERSITY'S CAMDEN CAMPUS FOR EIGHT YEARS AND DIRECTED THE URBAN LITERACY PROGRAM THROUGH WHICH HUNDREDS OF UNDERGRADUATES FROM ALL MAJORS TUTORED CHILDREN, YOUTH, AND ADULTS IN SCHOOLS, AGENCIES, AND THEIR OWN FAMILIES.

OTHER LITERACY TUTORS THAT LUCILLE HAS TRAINED INCLUDE :

- CHILDREN, YOUTH, AND PARENTS IN SUMMER-LONG LITERACY PROGRAMS IN A SOUTH CAMDEN HOUSING DEVELOPMENT;
- THIRD AND 8TH GRADERS IN REMEDIAL AND SPECIAL EDUCATION PROGRAMS;
- PARENTS OF CAMDEN SCHOOL CHILDREN;
- TEACHER MENTORS AND INSTRUCTIONAL AIDES;
- SPECIAL EDUCATION AND REMEDIAL TEACHERS;
- TEACHERS FROM JUVENILE INSTITUTIONS AND A FEDERAL PRISON;
- LVA-TRAINED INMATES AT NJ STATE PRISON, THE STATE'S MAXIMUM SECURITY FACILITY;
- AMERICORPS LITERACY TUTORS STATEWIDE.

AT RUTGERS-CAMDEN, LUCILLE TAUGHT LEARNING-TO-LEARN AND WRITING STRATEGIES TO UNDERPREPARED COLLEGE STUDENTS WITH THE EDUCATIONAL OPPORTUNITY FUND PROGRAM FOR TEN YEARS. SHE ALSO TAUGHT DEVELOPMENTAL READING FOR THE EDUCATION DEPARTMENT AND WAS A CURRICULUM DEVELOPMENT SPECIALIST IN A TEACHING EXCELLENCE CENTER JOINT VENTURE WITH A PUBLIC SCHOOL. SHE HAS TAUGHT OPEN ENROLLMENT ABE AND GED CLASSES FOR THE CAMDEN HOUSING AUTHORITY AND FOR DELAWARE TECHNICAL AND COMMUNITY COLLEGE. IN PHILADELPHIA, SHE WAS ON THE STAFF OF DREXEL UNIVERSITY'S STATE-FUNDED WORKFORCE DEVELOPMENT INSTITUTE, AND FOR FIVE YEARS SHE TAUGHT A GRADUATE COURSE IN CAREER COUNSELING AND DEVELOPMENT AT TEMPLE UNIVERSITY.

LUCILLE DID DOCTORAL-LEVEL WORK IN ADULT LITERACY AT THE FIELDING INSTITUTE, SANTA BARBARA, CA, UNDER THE MENTORSHIP OF THE LATE MALCOLM KNOWLES. SHE IS THE AUTHOR OF *EASY READER, LEARNER, WRITER: SIX VIDEOTAPES AND A TEACHER GUIDE* (AMERICAN GUIDANCE SERVICE, 1994); AND *VOICE HIDDEN, VOICE HEARD: A READING AND WRITING ANTHOLOGY* (KENDALL/HUNT, 1998).

THE TUTORING MINI-LOG
ALPHABET STRIPS
AND MINDMAPS
ON THE FOLLOWING PAGES
ARE DUPLICATED
TO ALLOW REMOVAL
FOR FURTHER DUPLICATION.

NO PERMISSION REQUIRED.

TUTORING LOG
An Easy Planning and Summary Chart
by Lucille T. Chagnon

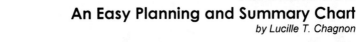

Learning Partner_____ Tel._____

Organization_____

Tutoring Location _____ Tel. _____

Meeting Time/Day _____ Tutor_____

To **plan** and **record** your tutoring session:
1. Write the date at the top of the first free column.
2. In that column, put a dot across from each of the things you plan to do.
3. To record what you did: After each tutoring session turn the relevant dots into check marks. Add check marks to other items covered.
4. On the back of this form, record the date, time spent, and anything significant that happened.

Dates:										
a. You read to them.										
b. Journal keeping / Free writing										
c. Mindmapping / Brainstorming										
d. Writing down their stories (LEA)										
e. Creating poetry or stories										
f. Exploring books										
g. Storytelling from Picture Books										
h. Silent reading										
i. They read to you.										
j. Decoding from context clues										
k. Decoding phonetically										
l. Word families, rhyming words										
m. Magazines, newspapers										
n. Learning at the computer										
o. Word games										
p. Four-level reflection										
q. Tutor training										
r. Other: Explain on reverse.										

No permission needed to reproduce this page.

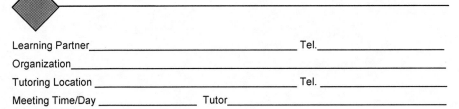

TUTORING LOG
An Easy Planning and Summary Chart
by Lucille T. Chagnon

Learning Partner_____ Tel._____

Organization_____

Tutoring Location _____ Tel. _____

Meeting Time/Day _____ Tutor_____

To **plan** and **record** your tutoring session:
5. Write the date at the top of the first free column.
6. In that column, put a dot across from each of the things you plan to do.
7. To record what you did: After each tutoring session turn the relevant dots into check marks. Add check marks to other items covered.
8. On the back of this form, record the date, time spent, and anything significant that happened.

Dates:											
a. You read to them.											
b. Journal keeping / Free writing											
c. Mindmapping / Brainstorming											
d. Writing down their stories (LEA)											
e. Creating poetry or stories											
f. Exploring books											
g. Storytelling from Picture Books											
h. Silent reading											
i. They read to you.											
j. Decoding from context clues											
k. Decoding phonetically											
l. Word families, rhyming words											
m. Magazines, newspapers											
n. Learning at the computer											
o. Word games											
p. Four-level reflection											
q. Tutor training											
r. Other: Explain on reverse.											

No permission needed to reproduce this page.

A B C D E F G H I J K L M N O P Q R S T U V W X Y Z

A B C D E F G H I J K L M N O P Q R S T U V W X Y Z

A B C D E F G H I J K L M N O P Q R S T U V W X Y Z

A B C D E F G H I J K L M N O P Q R S T U V W X Y Z

A B C D E F G H I J K L M N O P Q R S T U V W X Y Z

A B C D E F G H I J K L M N O P Q R S T U V W X Y Z

A B C D E F G H I J K L M N O P Q R S T U V W X Y Z

A B C D E F G H I J K L M N O P Q R S T U V W X Y Z

A B C D E F G H I J K L M N O P Q R S T U V W X Y Z

A B C D E F G H I J K L M N O P Q R S T U V W X Y Z

A B C D E F G H I J K L M N O P Q R S T U V W X Y Z

A B C D E F G H I J K L M N O P Q R S T U V W X Y Z

A B C D E F G H I J K L M N O P Q R S T U V W X Y Z

A B C D E F G H I J K L M N O P Q R S T U V W X Y Z

A B C D E F G H I J K L M N O P Q R S T U V W X Y Z

A B C D E F G H I J K L M N O P Q R S T U V W X Y Z

A B C D E F G H I J K L M N O P Q R S T U V W X Y Z

A B C D E F G H I J K L M N O P Q R S T U V W X Y Z

A B C D E F G H I J K L M N O P Q R S T U V W X Y Z

A B C D E F G H I J K L M N O P Q R S T U V W X Y Z

A B C D E F G H I J K L M N O P Q R S T U V W X Y Z

A B C D E F G H I J K L M N O P Q R S T U V W X Y Z

A B C D E F G H I J K L M N O P Q R S T U V W X Y Z

A B C D E F G H I J K L M N O P Q R S T U V W X Y Z

A B C D E F G H I J K L M N O P Q R S T U V W X Y Z

A B C D E F G H I J K L M N O P Q R S T U V W X Y Z

A B C D E F G H I J K L M N O P Q R S T U V W X Y Z

A B C D E F G H I J K L M N O P Q R S T U V W X Y Z

A B C D E F G H I J K L M N O P Q R S T U V W X Y Z

A B C D E F G H I J K L M N O P Q R S T U V W X Y Z

A B C D E F G H I J K L M N O P Q R S T U V W X Y Z

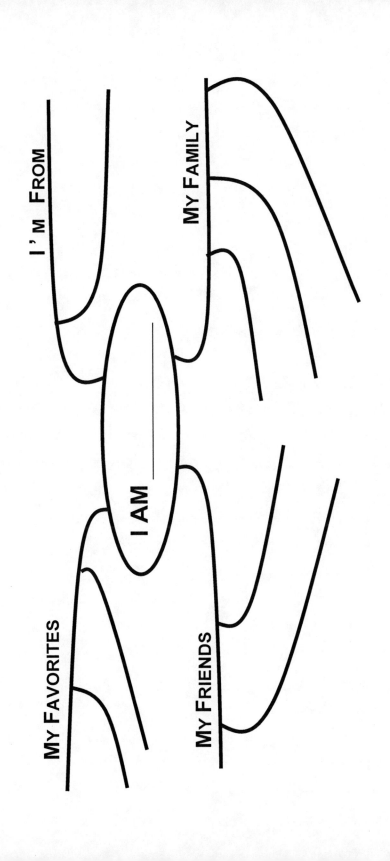

I'M FROM

MY FAMILY

I AM _____

MY FAVORITES

MY FRIENDS

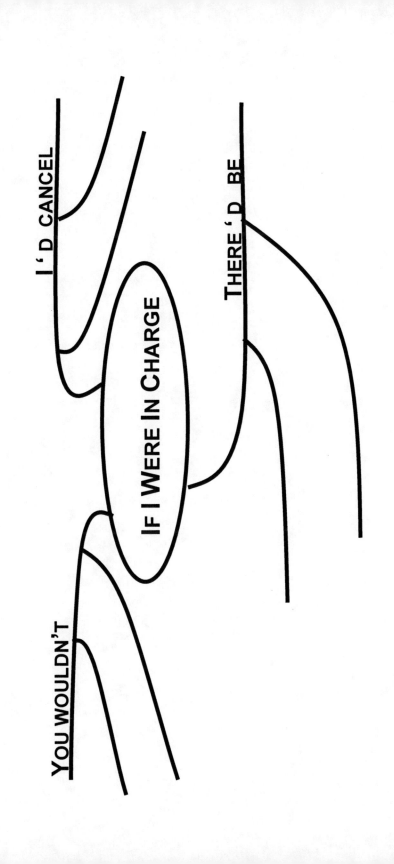

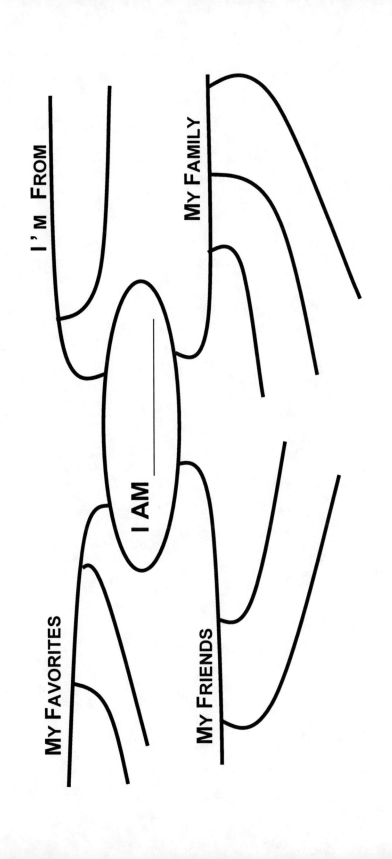

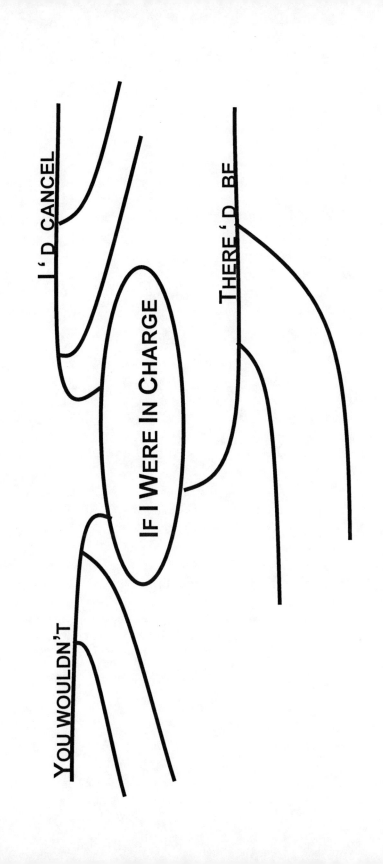

LaVergne, TN USA
15 April 2010
179342LV00002B/114/A